"ARE YOU PRACTICING
WHAT YOU PREACH?"

"ARE YOU PRACTICING WHAT YOU PREACH?"

IF NOT, HERE'S SOMETHING TO LIVE BY

BY TARSHA WORKS

Pictures by: Thomas with Big Visions, Saginaw, Michigan 48601
www.big-visions.com

Ahsrat Publishing, LLC.

P.O.Box 2464
Saginaw, MI 48605-2464

"Speaking the Truth about God, the Father, Jesus, his Son and the Holy Spirit"

ISBN 978-0-615-13344-7

0-615-13344-4

For Worldwide Distribution
Printed in the U.S.A

This book is available at Christian bookstores and distributors worldwide.

For more information on ordering this book direct, call
1-888-256-8419

Or reach us on the Internet:
www.tarshaworks.net

Dedication

I would like to give thanks to God, in which the Holy Spirit inspired me to write this book. I would like to thank my Mother, Sarah whom is very special to me and whom is my best friend for encouraging me to finish this book on time! A special thanks to my Father, Jerry for all his support. I love you both so very much! The following is a note of thanks to all that have my best interest and all my supporters: Shawn, thanks for all the encouraging words and thanks for being a great friend, God Bless! To all my extended family, my grandmother, Lela Calhoun, Jenny, Marion, to all the Works and Blakely family, Annie Ross, Willie Works, (C.J.) Carmelo Works, William Ross, and to all those I missed. I love you all. God Bless!

Tarsha Works
Ahsrat Publishing, LLC.
Saginaw, MI

Table of Contents

A Word of Explanation

Are You Practicing What You Preach? If Not, Here's
Something To Live By, is written to help spread the gospel
to the lost and non-believers as well as to help the captives
get set free and stay out of bondage. The goal is to stay
focused and on course for God, by practicing what you
preach. The key point here is to get everyone to understand
the importance of walking upright in the spirit and having a
one-on-one personal relationship with Jesus Christ.
Operating in the Spirit will show God that you are able to
put your flesh under subjection. To be spiritually discerned
is to know and understand the difference between the
things of God, which are good and the things of the devil
which are evil.   Also this book focuses on how to break
Generational Curses off your life. Last but not least, this
book explains about the importance of salvation and how to
really know if you are covered by the "Blood of Jesus"
until the day of redemption. Stay blessed by being
obedient to the Spirit of the Lord. Then watch God do a
great work in your life. May God's Holy Spirit fill you as
you worship God in spirit and in truth! Do not be afraid to
go out into the streets and preach the gospel to the lost!

LIVING THE LIFE

PROSPERITY

To be prosperous in everything by having

an abundance, overflow or increase.

SALVATION

To be saved. Accept Jesus as your saviour.

Repent of all your sins, turn from evil,

be baptized "IN THE NAME OF JESUS",

and you shall receive the gift of the Holy Ghost.

VIRTUOUS WOMAN OF GOD

Proverbs 31:10 reads, Who can find a virtuous woman? for her price is far above rubies. A Proverbs 31 woman of God who fears the Lord and loves her husband and will do him no harm. She is blessed.

Proverbs 31:30 Favor is deceitful, and beauty is vain: but a woman that feareth the Lord, she shall be praised.

HAVING AUTHORITY OVER THE DEVIL

Rebuke the devil in the "Name of Jesus"
and seal it with "The Blood of Jesus". The
devil cannot harm you if you are covered
by the blood! In order to be covered by the
"Blood of Jesus", you must be baptized
in Jesus name!

HOLY GHOST FILLED

Baptized in the Name of Jesus
and FILLED WITH THE HOLY
GHOST. Get filled today if you
do not already have the Holy Ghost!

BLESSINGS

An increase given from God when you are OBEDIENT to his Holy Word and Commandments. Proverbs 10:22 The blessing of the LORD, it maketh rich, and he addeth no sorrow with it.

FAITH *Hebrews 11:1 NOW faith is the substance of things hoped for, the evidence of things not seen.*

TRUTH *The word of God is the truth. To be honest, upfront, and "in the light" with no hidden agenda.*

LOVE *Being able to love God and in doing so, you can love others unconditionally.*

OBEDIENCE *Submitting to the authority of God.*

MANIFESTATION *Is when everything you speak out of your mouth into existence happens in your life at any given time.*

SATURATE YOURSELF WITH GOD'S WORD

ACCEPTING CHRIST AS YOUR PERSONAL SAVIOU

CHAPTER 1

"ARE YOU PRACTICING WHAT YOU PREACH?"

Even so hath the Lord ordained that they which preach the gospel should live of the gospel (I Corinthians 9:14).

"ARE YOU PRACTICING WHAT YOU PREACH?" IF NOT, HERE'S SOMETHING TO LIVE BY

This book is about how to live the same life that you are preaching to others about by not being a hypocrite. This is speaking to everyone from the leaders in the pulpit to the members in the pews. In addition, this book reveals to everyone about how to get set free from the life of strongholds and bondage. Once you finish reading this book, you will be able to recognize the works of the devil and his devices. The ultimate goal is to enlighten everyone about how to totally believe and trust in God for everything in life. So, please do not continue to be bound by the devil and have all your blessings blocked as a result of being disobedient to the word of God. There should be a point in life where a person should want to change their ways and live their life in a way that is pleasing in the sight of the Lord. Why? Heaven and hell are **REAL**!

Thou believest that there is one God; thou doest well: the devils also believe, and tremble (James 2:19).

Now if the devils believe and tremble because they know God is real, then why are people deceived and cannot believe in God? Do not be deceived by the cunning and craftiness of the devil. The devil has deceived many and he is still doing his job here in the earth. What is his job? The devils job is to seek whom he may devour.

> *Be sober, be vigilant; because your adversary the devil, as a roaring lion, walketh about, seeking whom he may devour* (I Peter 5:8):

Now that you know what the devils job is, there is no reason for you to be deceived anymore!

The only way for you not to be deceived by the devil is to actually live the life you are preaching about and not lie. Honestly, how do you expect for God to change your life if you are not willing to change by making the first step? If you are preaching the gospel then the word of God **"must hit you first"**. At this point, unbelievers may desire to change based upon seeing other worshippers of God, lead by example. The word of God is plain and simple. Do not add to the bible and do not take away from it. Accept the truth for what it is. Preach exactly what the word of God says. This will allow more deliverance to take place in the lives of others. The truth will keep a lot of people out of bondage once a "***RHEMA WORD***" is preached. A rhema word is a life changing word or message given to the Messenger by the Holy Spirit.   You must recognize that there is a Spiritual Warfare going on in the atmosphere and you must speak out against these forces by using your weapons of warfare which are, "the Blood of Jesus" and "the Name of Jesus." When you know who you are in God, you can move mountains by exercising and releasing your faith in God. Start thanking God for divine revelation and for his deliverance power. Once a person comes into the knowledge of the truth, he/she will be able to see with their spiritual eyes. No longer will a true worshipper be blinded by the powers of darkness of this world because they will be able to see the light. In order to stay in the light, once you accept Christ, you must walk in the light by constantly being in the presence of God. This means that everything you do must be honest in the sight of the Lord.

Are You Practicing What You Preach?

People are watching you at all times when you least expect it. God can see you as well! God will always allow a witness to see you if you are living a lie. Therefore, you must be Christ like in how you treat people once you become a member of the body of Christ. For those who do not know, as a member of the body of Christ, you are to preach the gospel of Jesus Christ! Once in a leadership role, you have to be careful how you live your life especially if you are a leader in church such as an, Apostle, Prophet, Pastor, Evangelist and/or a Teacher. The reason is because many souls are in the balance and what you preach, teach and say to someone will stick with them, just as well as what you do! Whatever is done in the dark, comes to the light and will be revealed some kind of way if you are not **PRACTICING WHAT YOU PREACH!** If what you are saying does not line up with what you are doing, then are you really practicing what you preach? Are you truly delivered from your sins? Shortcomings? Drama? All your idiosyncrasies? Are you really sure that you are delivered from all your sins before you start preaching to someone else about the truth? You must examine yourself first. It is a must that you make sure you are not living a lie. How can Satan cast out Satan? You have to live the truth like everyone else! It is important that when the word of God is delivered, you are operating in the Spirit so you can receive a powerful word from God that will bring forth deliverance. Some may be able to preach the word of God, but have no power. The word of God says in Acts 1:8 that you shall receive power after that the Holy Ghost is come upon you. If the Messenger is under the anointing of God, there will be deliverance, breakthroughs, healing and the captives will be set free. It is a MUST that you ask God for understanding of his word if you do not fully understand the bible when you read it. God will give you the ability to understand the bible for what it really is and God will also reveal the truth to all those that diligently seek his face.

IT IS IMPORTANT THAT YOU PRACTICE WHAT YOU PREACH BECAUSE GOD IS WATCHING!

Do not play with God.

> *Saying, Touch not mine anointed and, do my prophets no harm* (Psalms 105:15).

As a worshipper, you should not be deceived by imposters or false prophets if you are studying your bible daily and seeking God. Remember, no one can go to heaven or hell for you. The choice is yours in regards to where you want to spend eternity.

Rebuking The Unclean Spirit Released In The Church

No! It is NOT ok to have a wife and a girlfriend on the side. Marriage consists of **one man and one woman**! Period! It is not right to have adultery going on right in the house of God. Those who allow this type of activity to take place will have to answer to God! The spirit of adultery and fornication has been released in many churches, and it must be stopped! God is not pleased! It is time for ALL leaders in the church to wake up and be in tune to the Holy Spirit. Learn to let the Holy Spirit lead, teach and guide so that a "Life Changing word" can be taught.

> *BRETHREN, if a man be overtaken in a fault, ye which are spiritual, restore such an one in the spirit of meekness; considering thyself, lest thou also be tempted. Bear ye one another's burdens, and so fulfill the law of Christ* (Galatians 6:1-2).

It is a must to take authority over the devil by casting him out of the church, out of your households and out of your life for good. Get it right before it is too late! God is not pleased and pride goes before destruction. Do not be deceived by the devil and his deceitful workers of iniquity. Who sowed the tares, the devil.

> *Another parable put he forth unto them, saying, The kingdom of heaven is likened unto a man which sowed good seed in his field: But while men slept, his enemy came and sowed tares among the wheat, and went his way. But when the blade was sprung up, and brought forth fruit, then appeared the tares also. So the servants of the householder came and said unto him, Sir, didst not thou sow good seed in thy field? from whence then hath it tares? He said unto them, An enemy hath done this. The servants said unto him, Wilt thou then that we go and gather them up? But he said, Nay; lest while ye gather up the tares, ye root up also the wheat with them. Let both grow together until the harvest: and in the time of harvest I will say to the reapers, Gather ye together first the tares, and bind them in bundles to*

burn them: but gather the wheat into my barn
(Matthew 13:24-30).

*He answered and said unto them, He that soweth
the good seed is the Son of man; The field is the
world; the good seed are the children of the
kingdom; but the tares are the children of the
wicked one; The enemy that sowed them is the
devil; the harvest is the end of the world; and the
reapers are the angels. As therefore the tares are
gathered and burned in the fire; so shall it be in the
end of this world. The Son of man shall send forth
his angels and they shall gather out of his kingdom
all things that offend, and them which do iniquity;
And shall cast them into a furnace of fire: there
shall be wailing and gnashing of teeth. Then shall
the righteous shine forth as the sun in the kingdom
of their Father. Who hath ears to hear, let him
hear. Again, the kingdom of heaven is like unto
treasure hid in a field; the which when a man hath
found, he hideth, and for joy thereof goeth and
selleth all that he hath, and buyeth that field. Again,
the kingdom of heaven is like unto a merchant man,
seeking goodly pearls: Who, when he had found one*

pearl of great price, went and sold all that he had, and bought it. Again, the kingdom of heaven is like unto a net, that was cast into the sea, and gathered of every kind: Which, when it was full, they drew to shore, and sat down, and gathered the good into vessels, but cast the bad away. So shall it be at the end of the world: the angels shall come forth, and sever the wicked from among the just, And shall cast them into the furnace of fire: there shall be wailing and gnashing of teeth (Matthew 13: 37-50).

Please do not be like the wicked!

VERILY, verily, I say unto you, He that entereth not by the door into the sheepfold, but climbeth up some other way, the same is a thief and a robber. But he that entereth in by the door is the shepherd of the sheep. To him the porter openeth; and the sheep hear his voice: and he calleth his own sheep by name, and leadeth them out. And when he putteth forth his own sheep, he goeth before them, and the sheep follow him: for they know his voice.

And a stranger will they not follow, but will flee
from him: for they know not the voice of strangers
(John 10:1-5).

It is very important to know that God is your shepherd and
he knows his children. If you are on divine assignment and
have been instructed by the Holy Spirit, then it is important
that you say exactly what the Spirit of God is instructing
you to say to his people. Once you are in covenant with
God then you can hear his voice. So if God is not talking,
please do not lie on God because he is not talking to
everybody.

I have not sent these prophets, yet they ran: I have
not spoken to them, yet they prophesied (Jeremiah
23:21).

God is not pleased with the fact that there are so many
people using his name in vain and lying and saying that
"God said this" or **"God said that"**, when in all actuality,
God never spoke to them. In the last times there will arise
false prophets. This is the last times and it is happening
right before your eyes. People please know that when God
speaks to someone, he will always confirm his word.

HOW DO YOU GET INTO THE PRESENCE OF GOD?

Get into the presence of God by doing the following.
1. **Seek Gods face to get his attention.**
2. **Consecrate yourself by fasting and praying daily.**
3. **Meditate day and night on the scriptures in the bible.**
4. **Pray in the Holy Ghost. Speak to God in prayer in an unknown tongue once you receive the Holy Ghost.**

Once you get into the presence of God you will be able to obey and do exactly what the word of God is telling you to do. My advice is, do not be held captive ever again by the devil. For those of you who do not believe in Jesus today, your eyes will be opened and hopefully you will believe from receiving a revelation of the scriptures about God, which is the truth! From this point on, you will know the truth about God, his Son Jesus and the Holy Spirit which is the Comforter, who are all one. Everyone will find out if they do not already know, that God is a Spirit and they that worship him, "must worship him" in Spirit and in Truth!

God is a Spirit: and they that worship him must worship him in spirit and in truth (John 4:24).

Those who think the devil is not real, do not be deceived because he has many people blinded in their mind.

But their minds were blinded: for until this day remaineth the same vail untaken away in the reading of the old testament; which vail is done away in Christ. But even unto this day, when Moses is read, the vail is upon their heart. Nevertheless when it shall turn to the Lord, the vail shall be taken away. (II Corinthians 3:14-16).

In whom the god of this world hath blinded the minds of them which believe not, lest the light of the glorious gospel of Christ, who is the image of God, should shine unto them. For we preach not ourselves, but Christ Jesus the Lord; and ourselves your servants for Jesus' sake. For God, who commanded the light to shine out of darkness, hath shined in our hearts, to give the light of the knowledge of the glory of God in the face of Jesus Christ (II Corinthians 4:4-6).

27

It is time for the blinders to be taken off!

> *But he that hateth his brother is in darkness, and*
> *walketh in darkness, and knoweth not whither he*
> *goeth, because that darkness hath blinded his eyes*
> (I John 2:11).

To be blinded in the mind is being unable to accept the truth and see the light. Learn to embrace the truth. This book is giving bible scriptures to show validity about the truth by getting the message out to help the captives get set free from bondage. The time is now to worship the Lord and get your life together because God is, **I REPEAT, GOD IS COMING BACK!** Are you going to be ready? Tomorrow is not promised. Take a look in the newspaper and see how many people are dying daily. When I look at all the obituaries, I always say, "I hope they were saved." There are too many people dying. We do not know when it will be our time to pass on. Please let this be a wake up call and/or a reality check. Once that day comes when you no longer have the breath of life, there is not going to be a second chance in the flesh to get it right with God once he comes back. Remember Noah, how he kept saying, "it's going to rain", well God is coming back. So, why not get your life right today and trust in the Lord for everything, while the blood is still running warm in your veins.

> *But seek ye first the kingdom of God, and his righteousness; and all these things shall be added unto you* (Matthew 6:33).

> *Take therefore no thought for the morrow: for the morrow shall take thought for the things of itself. Sufficient unto the day is the evil thereof* (Matthew 6:34).

> *Whereas ye know not what shall be on the morrow. For what is your life? It is even a vapour, that appeareth for a little time, and then vanisheth away. For that ye ought to say, If the Lord will, we shall live, and do this, or that. But now ye rejoice in your boastings: all such rejoicing is evil. Therefore to him that knoweth to do good, and doeth it not, to him it is sin.* (James 4:14-17).

> *But my God shall supply all your need according to his riches in glory by Christ Jesus* (Philippians 4:19).

Once again, you can see the word of God for yourself. Take heed to the message. The kingdom of God is at hand. Therefore, I encourage you to get saved and receive the Holy Spirit before it is too late! If you are not sure that you are saved and have the Holy Ghost "with evidence of speaking in an unknown tongue", here is how to find out.

How do you know if you are saved?

1. **Believe that Jesus died on the cross for your sins that you might be saved.**
2. **Accept Jesus Christ into your life.**
3. **Repent of all your sins once you come into the knowledge of the truth about God and his Son Jesus Christ.**
4. **Be baptized in the name of Jesus and you shall receive the gift of the Holy Ghost.**

CHAPTER 2

THE BLOOD OF JESUS

And almost all things are by the law purged with blood; and without shedding of blood is no remission (Hebrews 9:22).

This is he that came by water and blood, even Jesus
Christ; not by water only, but by water and blood.
And it is the Spirit that beareth witness, because the
Spirit is truth. For there are three that bear record
in heaven, the Father, the Word, and the Holy
Ghost: and these three are one. And there are three
that bear witness in earth, the Spirit, and the water,
and the blood: and these three agree in one
(I John 5:6-8).

THE BLOOD OF JESUS

The blood of Jesus is what is going to cleanse you from all
unrighteousness. When you have been sealed with the
blood of Jesus, do not give the devil free course in your life
because you belong to God. The temptation from the devil
is still going to come but you have to realize that you have
the power to rebuke the devil "in the name of Jesus" as a
child of God.

And the seventy returned again with joy, saying,
Lord, even the devils are subject unto us through
thy name (Luke 10:17).

How do you know if you are covered by the **"BLOOD OF JESUS"**? If you are not sure, then this is how you find out. The first step is to acknowledge that you messed up in life and you strongly desire to change your life by submitting to God. Then, repent and turn from all your evil ways. Next, get baptized in the "Name of Jesus." Getting baptized in the name of Jesus is very important because this is the name that the devils recognize and are subject to. We all have sinned; so you must confess your sins in order to be cleansed from all unrighteousness. Then you are to be baptized in the water. The blood of Jesus is very powerful and can be used as one of your main "Weapons" when you wrestle against spiritual wickedness in high places. Please do not take a chance on not being covered by the blood. It is your right to have the blood covenant of Jesus!

> *This is the covenant that I will make with them after those days, saith the Lord, I will put my laws into their hearts, and in their minds will I write them; And their sins and iniquities will I remember no more. Now where remission of these is, there is no more offering for sin. Having therefore, brethren, boldness to enter into the holiest by the blood of Jesus, By a new and living way, which he hath*

consecrated for us, through the veil, that is to say,
his flesh; And having an high priest over the house
of God; Let us draw near with a true heart in full
assurance of faith, having our hearts sprinkled from
an evil conscience, and our bodies washed with
pure water. Let us hold fast the profession of our
faith without wavering; for he is faithful that
promised; (Hebrews 10:16-23).

Here is evidence of how to overcome the devil. Overcome
the devil by the blood of the Lamb and by the words of
your testimony. The key here is that your words have
power. There is power in what you say.

And the great dragon was cast out, that old serpent,
called the devil, and satan, which deceiveth the
whole world: he was cast out into the
earth, and his angels were cast out with him. And I
heard a loud voice saying in heaven, Now is come
salvation, and strength, and the kingdom of our
God, and the power of his Christ: for the accuser of
our brethren is cast down, which accused
them before our God day and night. And they
overcame him by the blood of the Lamb, and by the

word of their testimony; and they loved not their
lives unto the death (Revelation 12:9-11).

Based on the evidence of scripture backing, you should
now fully understand that there is power in the Blood of
Jesus. Jesus died on the cross for all our sins that we might
be saved.

PRAYER
Thank you Jesus that your precious blood has washed away
all my sins and I apply the blood of Jesus over my
life, in the name of Jesus that no weapon formed against me
shall prosper. I am more than a conqueror. Amen.

And from Jesus Christ, who is the faithful witness,
and the first begotten of the dead, and the prince of
the kings of the earth. Unto him that loved us, and
washed us from our sins in his own blood
(Revelation 1:5).

Scriptures to study regarding the "Blood of Jesus"

Hebrews 13:20, blood of the covenant
Acts 20:28, church purchased with his blood
John 6:54-56, drinketh my blood
I Corinthians 10:16, communion of blood of Christ
Colossians 1:14, redemption through his blood
Hebrews 9:22, without shedding of blood
Ephesians 1:7, redemption through his blood
Acts 17:26, made of one blood
I Peter 1:19, with precious blood of Christ
Hebrews 10:29, the blood of the covenant
Revelation 12:11, they overcame by the blood of the lamb

CHAPTER 3

WHO ARE YOU?

And we are his witnesses of these things; and so is also the Holy Ghost, whom God hath given to them that obey him (Acts 5:32).

He that believeth on the Son of God hath the witness in himself: he that believeth not God hath made him a liar; because he believeth not the record that God gave of his Son (I John 5:10-11).

WHO ARE YOU?

Do you really know who you are and how much power you actually have once you decide to put God first in your life? When you know who you are in Christ Jesus, a new boldness comes over your life which will allow you to be radical for Christ. All those who believe are considered to be the children of God. Are you Abraham's seed, heirs and joint heirs according to the promise? If you are, then start acting like it by having authority over the devil. Do you really know who you are? God gave you charge over the angels.

> *And if ye be Christ's, then are ye Abraham's seed, and heirs according to the promise* (Galatians 3:29).

> *ARE THEY NOT ALL MINISTERING SPIRITS, SENT forth to minister for them who shall be heirs of salvation?* (Hebrews 1:14).

> *Know ye not that ye are the temple of God, and that the Spirit of God dwelleth in you? If any man defile the temple of God, him shall God destroy; for the temple of God is holy, which temple ye are* (I Corinthians 3:16-17).

Then certain of the vagabond Jews, exorcists, took upon them to call over them which had evil spirits the name of the LORD Jesus, saying, we adjure you by Jesus whom Paul preacheth. And there were seven sons of one Sce'-va, a Jew, and chief of the priests, which did so. And the evil spirit answered and said, Jesus I know, and Paul I know; but who are ye? And the man in whom the evil spirit was leaped on them, and overcame them, and prevailed against them, so that they fled out of that house naked and wounded. And this was known to all the Jews and Greeks also dwelling at Eph'-e-sus; and fear fell on them all, and the name of the Lord Jesus was magnified. And many that believed came, and confessed, and shewed their deeds (Acts 19:13-18).

Unto the pure all things are pure: but unto them that are defiled and unbelieving is nothing pure; but even their mind and conscience is defiled. They profess that they know God; but in works they deny him, being abominable, and disobedient, and unto every good work reprobate (Titus 1:15-16).

But one in a certain place testified, saying, WHAT IS MAN THAT THOU ART MINDFUL OF HIM? OR THE SON OF MAN, THAT THOU VISITIEST HIM? THOU MADEST HIM A LITTLE LOWER THAN THE ANGELS; THOU CROWNEDST HIM WITH GLORY AND HONOR, AND DIDST SET HIM OVER THE WORKS OF THY HANDS: THOU HAST PUT ALL THINGS IN SUBJECTION UNDER HIS FEET. For in that he put all in subjection under him, he left nothing that is not put under him. But now we see not yet all things put under him (Hebrews 2:6-8).

When you know who you are in Christ Jesus the power inside of you will be made known and manifest. Once this happens, you will be able to speak things in your life into existence. At this point, you will have authority over the devil. Nothing will offend you and no one can deceive you once you understand the power you have inside. No longer will you be held captive. Then you will be able to tell the storm in your life to be still! Just as Jesus did when he calmed the storm.

And they came to him, and awoke him, saying,
Master, master, we perish. Then he arose, and
rebuked the wind and the raging of the water: and
they ceased, and there was a calm (Luke 8:24).

And he said unto them, Where is your faith? And
they being afraid wondered, saying one to another,
What manner of man is this for he commandeth
even the winds and water, and they obey him
(Luke 8:25).

Now you can begin to walk by faith and not by sight.
There will not be anything you cannot overcome once you
fully understand who you are in Christ Jesus. A new
boldness will overtake you when you recognize the power
you have in Christ Jesus. As children of God nothing can
touch you. No weapon formed against you shall prosper!

No weapon that is formed against thee shall
prosper; and every tongue that shall rise against
thee in judgment thou shalt condemn. This is the
heritage of the servants of the LORD, and their
righteousness is of me, saith the LORD
(Isaiah 54:17).

It is time for the real men and women of God to stand up! It is time for us to be serious about God because the kingdom of heaven is at hand. It is time for the true worshippers to stand up for God and practice what they preach. The time is now for you to start standing firm being steadfast and unmoveable in the word of God.

> *Therefore, my beloved brethren, be ye steadfast, unmoveable, always abounding in the work of the Lord, forasmuch as ye know that your labour is not in vain in the Lord.* (I Corinthians 15:58).

It is time for you to start casting out the devil by telling him to go back to hell because you know that the devil is already defeated! It is time out for the weakest link; meaning it is time out for that weak soldier in the army of the Lord claiming that he is a minister of God to sit down and let God's anointed and chosen complete his work. Why? There is a hurting and dying generation that does not even know about God or Jesus! The devil is so cunning and crafty that those who are not in Christ have no clue or knowledge of satan's devices. This is why so many are deceived.

For such are false apostles, deceitful workers,
transforming themselves into the apostles of Christ.
And no marvel; for Satan himself is transformed
into an angel of light. Therefore it is no great thing
if his ministers also be transformed as the ministers
of righteousness; whose end shall be according to
their works (II Corinthians 11:13-15).

It is time for the imposters to move so God's anointed can get in position to do the will of God. When you know who you are in God, no one will be able to come up against you, deceive, or tell you something that is a lie. You will have the power to discern between Good and evil by trying the spirits.

Beloved, believe not every spirit, but try the spirits
whether they are of God: because many false
prophets are gone out into the world (I John 4:1).

Hereby know we that we dwell in him, and he in us,
because he hath given us of his spirit. And we have
seen and do testify that the Father sent the son to be
the Saviour of the world. Whosoever shall confess

that Jesus is the Son of God, God dwelleth in him,
and he in God (I John 4:13-15).

And if it seem evil unto you to serve the Lord,
choose you this day whom ye will serve: whether
the gods which your fathers served that were on the
other side of the flood, or the gods, of the Am-or-
ites, in whose land ye dwell: but as for me and my
house, we will serve the Lord (Joshua 24:15).

Who are you? When you know who you are you can cast
out devils just as Jesus did.

And he said unto them, Go ye into all the world, and
preach the gospel to every creature. He that
believeth and is baptized shall be saved; but he that
believeth not shall be damned. And these signs
shall follow them that believe; In my name shall
they cast out devils; they shall speak with new
tongues; They shall take up serpents; and if they
drink any deadly thing, it shall not hurt them; they
shall lay hands on the sick, and they shall recover
(Mark 16:15-18).

Again, I ask – Who are you? A believer or a doubter?

But ye shall receive power, after that the Holy
Ghost is come upon you: and ye shall be witnesses
unto me both in Jerusalem, and in all Ju-dae'a, and
in Sa-ma'-ri-a, and unto the uttermost part of the
earth (Acts 1:8).

And they were all filled with the Holy Ghost, and
began to speak with other tongues, as the Spirit
gave them utterance (Acts 2:4).

And we are his witnesses of these things; and so is
also the Holy Ghost, whom God hath given to them
that obey him (Acts 5:32).

Little children, let no man deceive you: he that
doeth righteousness is righteous, even as he is
righteous. He that committeth sin is of the devil; for
the devil sinneth from the beginning. For this
purpose the Son of God was manifested, that he
might destroy the works of the devil. Whosoever is
born of God doth not commit sin; for his seed
remaineth in him: and he cannot sin, because he is

45

born of God. In this the children of God are manifest, and the children of the devil: whosoever doeth not righteousness is not of God, neither he that loveth not his brother (I John 3:7-10).

Who are you? No, you cannot serve two masters, God and the devil and expect to enter into the kingdom of God. Flesh and blood cannot inherit the kingdom of God. Read more in I Corinthians 15:50. Besides, if you are neither hot nor cold then you are lukewarm. If you are lukewarm, then God will spue you out of his mouth!

I know thy works, that thou art neither cold nor hot: I would thou wert cold or hot. So then because thou art lukewarm, and neither cold nor hot, I will spue thee out of my mouth (Revelation 3:15-16).

Again, I ask. Who Are You?

A double minded man is unstable in all his ways (James 1:8).

But be ye doers of the word, and not hearers only, deceiving your own selves (James1:22).

This scripture means to do what the word of God is instructing you to do. Most of the time, people tend to hear the word and not apply it to their life. Since you have read the scripture that specifically tells you to be doers of the word, you can now apply the word of God to your life.

But whoso looketh into the perfect law of liberty, and continueth therein, he being not a forgetful hearer, but a doer of the word, this man shall be blessed in his deed. If any man among you seem to be religious, and bridelth not his tongue, but deceiveth his own heart, this man's religion is vain (James 1:25-26).

So do not be religious. The religious spirit must cease! A religious spirit is not of God. The "Holy Ghost" is the only spirit that is of God! When people say, "I am going to have to lay down my religion", know that any religion that you can **"lay down"** and/or **"pick up"** is not of God. God is not "a specific religion"! There is no specific religion that can categorize who God really is. Read the entire book of Acts and you will find out more about God, Jesus and the Holy Ghost. God is a spirit. Anything that exalts itself above God is an idol, which is known as "idolatry". God is not mocked. Obey the word of God by doing exactly what it is instructing you to do!

> *Now the Spirit speaketh expressly, that in the latter times some shall depart from the faith, giving heed to seducing spirits, and doctrines of devils, Speaking lies in hypocrisy, having their conscience seared with a hot iron; Forbidding to marry, and commanding to abstain from meats, which God hath created to be received with thanksgiving of them which believe and know the truth* (I Timothy 4:1-3).

Who Are You?

Many people today are not considerate or caring to others. It seems as if, people do not have a conscious anymore in regards to how they treat other people. This is ironic because many people who attend church, say they are believers and have a form of godliness but they are double tongued. This can be compared to Dr. Jeckle and Mr. Hyde. I can only talk about what I have seen and experienced in life. It is really sad, because this type of behavior is preventing a lot of people from coming into the knowledge of the truth! The following scriptures describe what is exactly happening.

> *For men shall be lovers of their own selves,*
> *covetous, boasters, proud, blasphemers, disobedient*
> *to parents, unthankful, unholy, Without natural*
> *affection, trucebreakers, false accusers, incontinent,*
> *fierce, despisers of those that are good, Traitors,*
> *heady, highminded, lovers of pleasures more than*
> *lovers of God; Having a form of godliness but*
> *denying the power thereof: from such turn away.*
> *For of this sort are they which creep into houses,*
> *and lead captive silly women laden with sins, led*
> *away with divers lust, Ever learning, and never*
> *able to come to the knowledge of the truth. Now as*
> *Jan'-nes and Jam'bres withstood Moses, so do*
> *these also resist the truth: men of corrupt minds,*
> *reprobate concerning the faith* (II Timothy 3:2-8).
> *But evil men and seducers shall wax worse and*
> *worse, deceiving, and being deceived*
> (II Timothy 3:13).

Who are you? Are you of God or the devil? Who are you? Are you a real, true, faithful worshipper of God or are you a doubter? Without faith it is impossible to please the Lord.

> *Therefore if any man be in Christ, he is a new creature: old things are passed away; behold, all things are become new* (II Corinthians 5:17).

Who are you? It is time for you to take off the mask, stop perpetrating and be who you are inside. There is no need for you to try and be like everyone else. It is perfectly ok to be different. God knows exactly who you are. You cannot fool God. God can see you. He can see through the disguise that you have on. So I advise you to be exactly who God made you. Do not even think about being like someone else or living a double life, because when reality kicks in, you will understand that God is the only one who can fill the void in your life. Remember you must have faith in order to please God. FEAR is of the devil. **FAITH IS OF GOD!** Do you really know who you are?

> *Verily, verily, I say unto you, He that believeth on me, the works that I do shall he do also; and greater works than these shall he do; because I go unto my Father. And whatsoever ye shall ask in my name,*

that will I do, that the Father may be glorified in the
Son. If ye shall ask anything in my name, I will do
it. If ye love me, keep my commandments. Even the
Spirit of truth; whom the world cannot receive,
because it seeth him not, neither knoweth him: but
ye know him; for he dwelleth with you, and shall be
in you. At that day ye shall know that I am in my
Father, and ye in me, and I in you. But the
Comforter, which is the Holy Ghost, whom the
Father will send in my name, he shall teach you all
things, and bring all things to your remembrance,
whatsoever I have said unto you
(John 14:12-15, 17, 20,26).

Great peace have they which love thy law: and
nothing shall offend them (Psalms119:165).

Are your works good or evil? When you pray to God,
know that you cannot hide who you are because God
knows you by name. When you go to God, you must take
all the bad things about you whether if you are a liar,
adulterer, fornicator, murderer, you must take all your
habits, all the things that are against the word of God and
give it to him, so he can change and use you for his

purpose. The word of God is not going to come back to him void. God is not a man that he should lie nor the Son of man that he should repent. This is biblical. When your heart is right with God, he will change you and make you whole. If any man be in Christ he is a new creature. Believe it and receive it. When you go to God you must remember that God looks on the inner man of your heart, not on the outer man of your appearance. If you want God to change you by coming into your life and making a difference, then just be sincere with God. Go ahead and make the first step and watch how God will begin to move in your life. The bible says that the steps of a good man are ordered by the Lord. This is why you must ask yourself the question, "Who am I"? I found out that when you know who you are in God you can move mountains, tread upon serpents, cast out devils, lay hands on the sick and they shall recover. Knowing who you are in Christ Jesus will take you very far in life once you accept Jesus Christ and get saved.

PRAYER

Lord, I believe in my heart and accept you Jesus Christ as my Lord and I shall be saved. Thank you God! I repent of all my sins and I ask you on this day to put all of my sins under the blood and remember them no more. Now, I can be baptized in the name of Jesus for the remission of sins and I shall receive the gift of the Holy Ghost, just like the bible says in Acts 2:38. I thank you God and I love you. Amen.

Scriptures to study for a "closer walk" with God

I John 5:19, we know that we are of God
II Timothy 3:5, a form of godliness
I Corinthians 14:25, that God is in you
Mark 12:32, one God, and none other
Romans 3:4, let God be true
Hebrews 8:10, I will be to them a God
Romans 8:31, if God be for us
I John 1:5, God is light
II Corinthians 7:9-10, godly sorrow worketh repentance
Luke 13:3, except ye repent
Acts 8:22, repent of this thy wickedness
Revelation 2:21, space to repent, and she repented not
Luke 17:3, if thy brother repent, forgive him
Psalms 91, dwelleth in the secret place of the most High
II Corinthians 7:1, perfecting holiness in fear of God

FORGIVENESS HEALS A BROKEN HEART

Forgiveness heals broken hearts. Try it. It really works. If you forgive everybody in your life, you will have Gods attention because he will forgive you for all your sins. Think of how many times you get down on your knees and pray to God but nothing seems to happen. At this point, you should reflect back over your life and think about all the people you have not forgiven. Try it. You have to forgive those people and release all the anger, hurt and all the pain in order to successfully function in life and move to the next level. Have you ever wondered why things do not go the way you plan it in your life? Well, it may be because there is some unforgiveness in your heart. Examine yourself to find out if there is any unforgiveness in your heart.

> *Judge not, and ye shall not be judged: condemn not, and ye shall not be condemned: forgive, and ye shall be forgiven:* (Luke 6:37).

Try to forgive today and watch God show up in your life.

Discussing the Spiritual Realm

What is the Spiritual Realm? The Spiritual Realm is the realm of the air in which you wrestle everyday with spiritual principalities. You must be equipped with the right weapons of warfare in order to overcome.

> *For we wrestle not against flesh and blood, but against principalities, against powers, against the rulers of the darkness of this world, against spiritual wickedness in high places* (Ephesians 6:12).

Many of your blessings are caught up in the Spiritual Realm. How do you get your blessings released from the spiritual realm? First, as a child of God, you must be obedient to the word of God. This is the key toward getting your blessings released from the Spiritual Realm. Second, you must have faith and believe.

> *NOW faith is the substance of things hoped for, the evidence of things not seen* (Hebrews 11:1).

But without faith it is impossible to please him: for he that cometh to God must believe that he is, and that he is a rewarder of them that diligently seek him (Hebrews 11:6).

But to which of the angels said he at any time, SIT ON MY RIGHT HAND, UNTIL I MAKE THINE ENEMIES THY FOOTSTOOL? Are they not all ministering spirits, sent forth to minister for them who shall be heirs of salvation? (Hebrews 1:13-14).

Obey God and turn to the truth! This is the only way to be set free. Here is proof.

As it is written in the law of Moses, all this evil is come upon us: yet made we not our prayer before the Lord our God, that we might turn from our iniquities, and understand thy truth. Therefore hath the Lord watched upon the evil, and brought it upon us: for the Lord our GOD is righteous in all his works which he doeth: for we obeyed not his voice (Daniel 9:13-14).

It is vital to be mindful of the words of Daniel. Be enlightened once again that there is power in your words. Also, note that the prince of Persia is waiting to block your words in any kind of way possible. Who is the prince of Persia? The prince of Persia is a king of any city set out to block the righteous. Read more about it in Daniel 10.

Daniels Words

> *And, behold, a hand touched me, which set me upon my knees and upon the palms of my hands. And he said unto me, O Daniel, a man greatly beloved, understand the words that I speak unto thee, and stand upright: for unto thee am I now sent. And when he had spoken this word unto me, I stood trembling. Then said he unto me, Fear not, Daniel: for from the first day that thou didst set thine heart to understand, and to chasten thyself before thy God, thy words were heard, and I am come for thy words. But the prince of the kingdom of Persia withstood me one and twenty days: but, lo, Mi'-cha-el, one of the chief princes, came to help me; and I remained there with the kings of Persia. Now I am come to make thee understand what shall befall thy*

people in the latter days: for yet the vision is for
many days (Daniel 10:10-14).

If you ask anything according to God's will, you have the petition to receive whatever you ask. You have not because you ask not. The word of God cannot return back to him void.

So shall my Word be that goeth forth out of my
mouth, it shall not return unto me void, but it shall
accomplish that which I please, and it shall prosper
in the thing whereto I sent it (Isaiah 55:11).

And also remember, you cannot live any kind of way and think God is going to give you what you want in life. It does not work this way! You have to be obedient to the word of God. If you keep the commandments of God, then God will give you the desires of your heart. The blessings of the Lord maketh rich and he added no sorrow with it. All things are possible to them that believe.

Forgiveness Prayer

Lord Jesus, I ask you to forgive me for all the people I have not forgiven. I have an open heart to forgive them right now Lord and I also ask you Lord to forgive me right now of all my sins. Create in me a clean heart and renew a right spirit in me Jesus. I come to you with sincerity in my heart and I know that your word says in I John 1:9, If we confess our sins, he is faithful and just to forgive us our sins, and to cleanse us from all unrighteousness. Thank you Jesus for cleansing me and I will obey your holy word in Jesus name. Amen.

"Tears Cried to God"

Jesus knows all about your troubles. He definitely knows of all the tears you cry. When it seems like you have done all that you can do in life, sometimes the only thing you really can do is stand still and believe God. Do not give up or give in. The race is given to the one that endures until the end. Stand on Gods word, when you think you cannot go on any further in life. When you feel like you want to give up and throw in the towel, stand on Gods word! Remember that it is perfectly fine to cry. I am sure that you have spent many nights crying and praying to God. Over time, God will release you from everything you are going through in life and bless you with double for all your trouble. God will work things out for his people who believe in him, just do not give up on God. He is alive and real. Let go of what is holding you down and release all of the past hurts, pains and look to God. Go ahead and let God clean you up. Let it go! What do you have to lose? Try Jesus! Stop looking for love in all the wrong places. Take your eyes off of everything else and see GOD! God is trying to get "your attention", so his will can be done in the earth. It is evident that God must have a vessel to use in order for him to have his word of truth to manifest in the earth. God knows exactly what is best for you because he is the creator of all mankind. God will never put more on you than you can bear. Release everything that is holding you back in life, so God can purge you and make you whole.

Release the past and look to God!

WALKING THE STRAIGHT AND NARROW

It is better to do what is right now by God, than for you to be in the judgment seat with God later. There will not be any blaming or pointing fingers at anyone because you are going to be held responsible for your own actions. It is not going to be momma, daddy, sister, brother, children, wife, husband or the Pastors fault. It will be your own fault if you are not obeying the word of God! Start today by walking the strait and narrow.

> *Therefore all things whatsoever ye would that men should do to you, do ye even so to them: for this is the law and the prophets. Enter ye in at the strait gate: for wide is the gate, and broad is the way, that leadeth to destruction, and many there be which go in thereat: Because strait is the gate, and narrow is the way, which leadeth unto life, and few there be that find it. Beware of false prophets, which come to you in sheep's clothing, but inwardly they are ravening wolves. Ye shall know them by their fruits. Do men gather grapes of thorns, or figs of thistles?* (Matthew 7:12-16).

CHAPTER 4

DISCUSSING SPIRITUAL WARFARE

For we wrestle not against flesh and blood, but against principalities, against powers, against the rulers of the darkness of this world, against spiritual wickedness in high places (Ephesians 6:12).

"Discussing Spiritual Warfare"

In the world today there are many different kinds of spirits, some good, bad and the other spirits you really cannot discern. Spirits are real. There is a Spiritual Warfare going on between good and evil in the earth today. What are you going to do about it? This is how one can overcome evil by **"showing love and doing that which is good in the sight of the Lord"**, not in the sight of men. How do you fight in a Spiritual Warfare?

How to fight in a Spiritual Warfare

1. Realize and understand that it is a spiritual warfare and that it is impossible to fight a spiritual battle with natural weapons. It will not work! I tried it! In order to win in a spiritual warfare you must fight by intercessory prayer and by fasting. To fast means to seek God for direction.

2. Rebuke and cast down every imagination that is not of God.

3. Pray in the spirit and intercede for the lost.

4. Put on the whole armour of God and stay steadfast and unmoveable in the word of God.

5. Believe that you can cast out devils because you are a child of God.

6. Pray out loud and speak against all unclean spirits by rebuking the spirits in the name of Jesus.

7. Humble yourself before God.

8. Do not be deceived by the devil.

9. Learn how to discern between good and evil.

10. Pray that God gives you the Spirit of discernment if you do not already have it.

Finally, my brethren, be strong in the Lord, and in the power of his might. Put on the whole armour of God, that ye may be able to stand against the wiles of the devil. For we wrestle not against flesh and blood, but against principalities, against powers, against the rulers of the darkness of this world, against spiritual wickedness in high places. Wherefore take unto you the whole armour of God, that ye may be able to withstand in the evil day, and having done all, to stand. Stand therefore, having your loins girt about with truth, and having on the breastplate of righteousness; And your feet shod with the preparation of the gospel of peace; Above all, taking the shield of faith, wherewith ye shall be able to quench all the fiery darts of the wicked. And take the helmet of salvation, and the sword of the

Spirit, which is the word of God: Praying always with all prayer and supplication in the Spirit, and watching thereunto with all perseverance and supplication for all saints; And for me, that utterance may be given unto me, that I may open my mouth boldly, to make known the mystery of the gospel, For which I am an ambassador in bonds: that therein I may speak boldly, as I ought to speak (Ephesians 6:10-20).

And these signs shall follow them that believe; In my name shall they cast out devils; they shall speak with new tongues; (Mark 16:17).

NOW the Spirit speaketh expressly, that in the latter times some shall depart from the faith, giving heed to seducing spirits, and doctrines of devils; Speaking lies in hypocrisy; having their conscience seared with a hot iron; Forbidding to marry, and commanding to abstain from meats, which God hath created to be received with thanksgiving of them which believe and know the truth (I Timothy 4:1-3).

To open their eyes, and to turn them from darkness to light, and from the power of Satan unto God, that they may receive forgiveness of sins, and inheritance among them which are sanctified by faith that is in me (Acts 26:18).

For it is impossible for those who were once enlightened, and have tasted of the heavenly gift, and were made partakers of the Holy Ghost, And have tasted the good word of God, and the powers of the world to come, If they shall fall away, to renew them again unto repentance; seeing they crucify to themselves the Son of God afresh, and put him to an open shame (Hebrews 6: 4-6).

Do not think for a second just because you are saved by the grace of God that you can live your life any kind of way. No! That is a lie because you belong to God and your spirit has to be accounted for once God calls you home. Every soul will either be accounted for unto GOD or in hell unto the devil. Today, literally it is up to you to make the decision about whom to serve. Will you serve God? Or will you serve the devil which is also known as, the prince of the power of the air? Who will you yield your members to? When you finally get the revelation in your mind, you will realize exactly how powerful the word of God is and can be in your life once you submit to God. There is also power in the NAME OF JESUS! When you have Jesus on your side, nothing is impossible! The key is that you must first believe, receive and then let the manifestation of God's holy word abide in your life.

> *Submit yourselves therefore to God. Resist the devil, and he will flee from you. Draw nigh to God, and he will draw nigh to you. Cleanse your hands, ye sinners; and purify your hearts, ye double minded* (James 4:7-8).

An important fact is that your body is the temple of the Holy Ghost. For those of you who like to see scripture like myself, here it is.

> *Know ye not that the unrighteous shall not inherit the kingdom of God? Be not deceived: neither fornicators, nor idolaters, nor adulterers, nor effeminate, nor abusers of themselves with mankind, nor thieves, nor covetous, nor drunkards, nor*

revilers, nor extortioners, shall inherit the kingdom
of God. And such were some of you: but ye are
washed, but ye are sanctified, but ye are justified in
the name of the Lord Jesus, and by the Spirit of our
God. All things are lawful unto me, but all things
are not expedient: all things are lawful for me, but
I will not be brought under the power of any. Meats
for the belly, and the belly for meats: but God shall
destroy both it and them. Now the body is not for
fornication, but for the Lord; and the Lord for the
body. And God hath both raised up the Lord, and
will also raise up us by his own power. Know ye
not that your bodies are the members of Christ?
Shall I then take the members of Christ, and make
them the members of an harlot? God forbid.
What? know ye not that he which is joined to an
harlot is one body? for two, saith he, shall be one
flesh. But he that is joined unto the Lord is one
spirit. Flee fornication. Every sin that a man doeth
is without the body; but he that committeth
fornication sinneth against his own body. What?
know ye not that your body is the temple of the Holy
Ghost which is in you, which ye have of God, and ye
are not your own? For ye are bought with a price:

therefore glorify God in your body, and in your spirit, which are God's (I Corinthians 6:9-20).

It is a blatent sin and a slap in the face to be disobedient to God and do everything under the sun. If you love God, then you will obey his word by keeping his commandments.

For if we sin willfully after that we have received the knowledge of the truth, there remaineth no more sacrifice for sins, (Hebrews 10:26).

HOW TO RESIST THE DEVIL

1. Rebuke the unclean spirit in the name of Jesus.
2. Ask God to forgive you by repenting and turning from your evil ways.
3. Saturate yourself in the word of God daily.
4. Pray and keep your mind stayed on the Lord.
5. Have faith in God.
6. Pray in the Holy Spirit.
7. Vindicate yourself from people who are negative and do not have your best interest until you are strong enough to witness to them.
8. Stay away from seducing spirits.

*And, behold, there was a woman which had a spirit
of infirmity eighteen years, and was bowed
together, and could in no wise lift up herself. And
when Jesus saw her, he called her to him, and said
unto her, Woman, thou art loosed from thine
infirmity. And he laid his hands on her: and
immediately she was made straight, and glorified
God. And the ruler of the synagogue answered with
indignation, because that Jesus had healed on the
Sabbath say, and said unto the people, There are six
days in which men ought to work: in them therefore
come and be healed, and not on the Sabbath day.
The Lord then answered him, and said, Thou
hypocrite, doth not each one of you on the sabbath
loose his ox or his ass from the stall, and lead him
away to watering? And ought not this woman, being
a daughter of Abraham, whom Satan hath bound, lo
these eighteen years, be loosed from this bond on
the sabbath day?* (Luke 13:11-16).

Satan has an assignment to discourage everyone who
believes in God. His plan is to kill, steal and destroy
anything that is in the image of God. The devil talks
people into doing things by coming into their mind with

thoughts! These thoughts can cause strain and stress on your life. Stop letting the devil come into your mind! So keep your mind focused on God.

> *Who hath delivered us from the power of darkness, and hath translated us into the kingdom of his dear Son:* (Colossians 1:13).

> *And the very God of peace sanctify you wholly; and I pray God your whole spirit and soul and body be preserved blameless unto the coming of our Lord Jesus Christ* (I Thessalonians 5:23).

> *Lest Satan should get an advantage of us: for we are not ignorant of his devices* (II Corinthians 2:11).

Remember that when you do not obey the word of God, you give the devil a green light to come in your life. The only way you can stop the devil is by obeying the word of God. Please understand that it is very important to obey the word of God and learn to hear the voice of God. In summary you resist the devil by establishing a relationship with God and giving reverence to the spirit of the Lord.

Recognizing Seducing Spirits and How to Keep Them Away From You

> *But we know that the law is good, if a man use it lawfully; Knowing this, that the law is not made for a righteous man, but for the lawless and disobedient, for the ungodly and for sinners, for unholy and profane, for murderers of fathers and murderers of mothers, for manslayers, For whoremongers, for them that defile themselves with mankind, for menstealers, for liars, for perjured persons, and if there be any other thing that is contrary to sound doctrine; (I Timothy 1:8-10).*

Seducing spirits really do exist. When you recognize a seducing spirit, you must bind it in the name of Jesus because it can overtake you if you are not careful.

> *NOW the Spirit speaketh expressly, that in the latter times some shall depart from the faith, giving heed to seducing spirits, and doctrines of devils; Speaking lies in hyprocrisy; having their conscience seared with a hot iron; (I Timothy 4:1-2).*

Once you are free from the seducing spirits that had you in bondage, it is important not to go back and get entangled with those spirits again. The reason is because the seducing spirits will try to latch back on and create another stronghold that will try to hold you back from what God has for you in life. This type of spirit or spirits can come back in many forms. If you have any trinklets, or items given to you as a gift, items passed down to you from other generations through a family member; such as clothing, rings, jewelry, books, shoes, horoscope, astrology signs, paraphernalia, etc. get rid of it because these items can carry spirits with them that are considered to be a green light for the devil to come into your life. Once you break the spirit, do not get entangled with that bondage again.

> *And many that believed came, and confessed, and shewed their deeds. Many of them also which used curious arts brought their books together, and burned them before all men: and they counted the price of them, and found it fifty thousand pieces of silver* (Acts 19:18-19).

How to Keep Seducing Spirits Away

1. You must speak out loud and confess the word of God with authority.
2. Read your bible daily.
3. Pray, pray, pray!

When you understand how to keep the seducing spirits away, you will not be bound and let the devil get the best of you ever again. In order for this to happen, you must begin to be bold and radical by taking a stand for yourself and rebuke the seducing spirits. Many people who walk this earth are held captive by seducing spirits. The sad part about it is that they do not even know it. The reason they do not know it or understand is because they might not be studying the word of God. It has been proven that anything that becomes controlling is a Spirit. There have been many cases where seducing spirits have infiltrated the person by causing them to be in denial. This is why it is so important to speak in tongues, which is called "Praying in the Spirit" to God, because your hearts pray to God.

> *For he that speaketh in an unknown tongue*
> *speaketh not unto men, but unto God: for no man*

understandeth him; howbeit in the spirit he
speaketh mysteries (I Corinthians 14:2).

When you pray to God from your heart, the devil does not understand what is being spoken. This is excellent because the devil will not be able to block your prayers. Therefore, please be aware of the seducing spirits that come about and try to overtake you when you least expect it. Do not be fooled or deceived by anyone because God is not the author of confusion and no sin is of God. Sin is of the devil in which evil is all in his name. When you are tempted, it is because of your own lusts.

> *But every man is tempted, when he is drawn away*
> *of his own lusts, and enticed. Then when lust hath*
> *conceived, it bringeth forth sin: and sin, when it is*
> *finished, bringeth forth death. Do not err, my*
> *beloved brethren.* (James 1:14-16).

The devil is a liar. Start taking authority over the devil by rebuking him "in the name of Jesus"! When you use the name of Jesus, the devil will flee from you because there is power in the name of Jesus. Glory to God! If you start rebuking the devil right now in the name of Jesus, I guarantee you that you will feel the power and start seeing a difference in your life that you have never experienced before. At this moment, you will realize and see exactly how much power you have as a worshipper and a believer of God. If you believe, anything is possible when you start using "the name of Jesus"!

PRAYER

Thank you Jesus for my health, life, strength and for faith. Thank you that the chains of darkness are broken, they have no rule or dominion over my life anymore. Thank you Jesus that I am free from darkness and brought into the light. I thank you Jesus that your ministering angels are now watching over me and my family and protecting us from any harm. I claim everything as being done in my life today in Jesus name. Amen, Thank God!

ARE YOU IN GOD'S PERFECT WILL OR PERMISSIVE WILL?

Are you in Gods perfect will or permissive will?

If you believe in God, your main focus here in the earth should be to worship God. Do you take time out of your busy schedule to stop and just say, "THANK YOU JESUS? Life is too short and God will give you a reality check when you are off course and not in his "perfect will" for your life. Yes, you can be in the will of God, even in God's permissive will for your life. There is none greater than for you to be in God's Perfect Will. It took me a while to figure this one out so let me give everyone some simple advice to figure out if you are in God's perfect will or not. I will start out by talking briefly about my experience. Pay close attention to my experience because what God is doing in my life, he can do the same in your life as well. All things are possible to them that believe. Do you really believe?

> *And be not conformed to this world: but be ye transformed by the renewing of your mind, that ye may prove what is that good, and acceptable, and perfect, will of God* (Romans 12:2).

MY EXPERIENCE

It all started when I first accepted Jesus Christ into my life back when I was seven years old. I knew many scriptures by heart but did not quite understand how to apply the word of God to my life. As time went on, I would always read the scriptures and say things out loud that I wanted to do in life and it would actually happen. Again, I still was not aware of the fact that, there were several scriptures that backed up everything that was happening for me in life and I was certain that God was with me! I never knew of the scripture in Proverbs 18:21. It was not until I became much older and more savvy in the word of God.

> *Death and life are in the power of the tongue: and they that love it shall eat the fruit thereof* (Proverbs 18:21).

I was aware at a very young age that there is power in the tongue. There is power in what you say and once you speak something into existence it shall come to pass. As time went on throughout my life, I experienced many trials and tests. After surviving two major car accidents, now I totally understand that my life has purpose. I tried to figure out why this was happening in my life or why that had to happen in my life, instead of just being thankful to God that my situation was not any worse. Now, I always give reverence and thanks to God and his Son Jesus every chance I get because I realize that God did not have to let me live. Thank God for his mercy, grace and for sparing my life each and every day. When people finally come to the conclusion that God is in control and they are not, this is when God has your attention and can come into your life and do a great work. I know without a shadow of doubt that all things happen for a reason and God has already predestined and ordained everything to happen just the way it did. Nothing happens by coincidence. There is a time and a season for everything. Please do not take as long as I did to figure it out! It is easy. All you have to do is submit to God, have faith and believe. This is the first couple of steps, the rest is going to occur based on your faith and how well you can put your flesh under subjection! There is a constant struggle with the flesh and the spirit. The flesh and the spirit are at war because the flesh is warring against the spirit.

> *THERE is therefore now no condemnation to them which are in Christ Jesus, who walk not after the flesh, but after the Spirit. For the law of the Spirit*

of life in Christ Jesus hath made me free from the law of sin and death. For what the law could not do, in that it was weak through the flesh, God sending his own Son in the likeness of sinful flesh, and for sin, condemned sin in the flesh: That the righteousness of the law might be fulfilled in us, who walk not after the flesh, but after the Spirit. For they that are after the flesh do mind the things of the flesh; but they that are after the Spirit the things of the Spirit. For to be carnally minded is death; but to be spiritually minded is life and peace. Because the carnal mind is enmity against God: for it is not subject to the law of God, neither indeed can be. So then they that are in the flesh cannot please God. But ye are not in the flesh, but in the Spirit, if so be that the Spirit of God dwell in you. Now if any man have not the Spirit of Christ, he is none of his. And if Christ be in you, the body is dead because of sin; but the Spirit is life because of righteousness. But if the Spirit of him that raised up Jesus from the dead dwell in you, he that raised up Christ from the dead shall also quicken your mortal bodies by his Spirit that dwelleth in you (Romans 8:1-11).

It is impossible to please God in the flesh. This is why it is so important for those who believe in God to be real and to worship God in spirit and in truth! I cannot stress this enough. God is not pleased with you living and acting any kind of way. There has to be a point in your life when you must say, I give Lord. Then you will be able to totally surrender and commit your life to God. When you make the first step, then God can manifest in your life. Go ahead today and make the choice. It is time for you to be real with God and stop straddling the fence. In order to truly worship God, you must be obedient to the word of God!

Scriptures about "obedience" to God

Acts 5:29, obey God rather than men
Romans 5:19, by the obedience of one
II Thessalonians 1:8, them that obey not the gospel
I Peter 1:22, purified your souls in obeying the truth
Hebrews 5:8, yet learned he obedience
Isaiah 1:19, if obedient ye shall eat
II Corinthians 2:9, obedient in all things
I Peter 1:2, unto obedience
Romans 16:19, your obedience is come
II Corinthians 10:5, thought to the obedience of Christ

CHAPTER 5

RELATIONSHIPS AND MARRIAGE

Marriage is honorable in all, and the bed undefiled: but whoremongers and adulterers God will judge (Hebrews 13:4).

Relationships and Marriage

As I begin to discuss the topic of marriage, I want to start off by speaking on relationships. To keep the entire subject in context I want to define the word relationship. Relationship is when two people engage in a friendship or a mutual agreement and get to know each other and/or build a friendship. There is no right or wrong way to describe the terminology "relationship". But what I would like to start off with is to actually introduce the most important relationship that must first be established and that is with "God". When one engages in a personal relationship with God before marriage, this allows the individual to be molded, shaped, pruned and prepared for the journey of marriage with their spouse. By establishing a relationship with God this entitles an individual to find out a whole lot of things about themselves and this also gives you a chance to fix some of the things you do not quite like about yourself, with the help of God. Remember that your spouse is not your God when you are in the marriage. No matter what, you still must keep God first in your life.

> *There is difference also between a wife and a virgin. The unmarried woman careth for the things of the Lord, that she may be holy both in body and in*

spirit: but she that is married careth for the things
of the world, how she may please her husband
(I Corinthians 7:34).

God honors marriage.

Marriage is honorable in all, and the bed undefiled:
but whoremongers and adulterers God will judge
(Hebrews 13:4).

Marriage is the union of one man and one woman!
The bible does not say to have more than one wife or more
than one husband.

Wives, submit yourselves unto your own husbands,
as unto the Lord. For the husband is the head of
the wife, even as Christ is the head of the church:
and he is the saviour of the body. Therefore as the
church is subject unto Christ, so let the wives be to
their own husbands in every thing. Husbands, love
your wives, even as Christ also loved the church,
and gave himself for it; That he might sanctify and
cleanse it with the washing of water by the word
(Ephesians 5:22-26).

Once a man and a woman come together in marriage, they become one with each other. There is an order that must be followed in marriage. The union between God who is first. Then, the husband, who is the head of the wife, and then the wife.

> *For this cause shall a man leave his father and mother, and shall be joined unto his wife, and they two shall be one flesh* (Ephesians 5:31).

To all single women, it is not your role to find a man. Focus on developing a personal relationship with the Lord.

> *Whoso findeth a wife findeth a good thing, and obtaineth favour of the Lord* (Proverbs 18.22).

Stop allowing people to manipulate you by twisting the scriptures for their own benefit. Obey the laws of the land. There is no such marriage that involves woman and woman or man and man. This is called an abomination to God. An abomination is anything that is against God.

> *Thou shalt not lie with mankind, as with womankind: it is abomination* (Leviticus 18:22).

Why do men and women lie to each other and say they are in love and in all actuality, they are not? It is concluded that, if God is invited into the relationships and marriages, maybe the union would be taken more seriously and would actually work out. This all depends on if the two people are equally yoked. Marriage is a challenge but each person should aim to give 100% each and be honest about everything no matter how much the truth might hurt.
Seek God in all that you do. I am just trying to keep it real, help somebody "get set free", get out and "stay out" of bondage. Once you get set free, do not be entangled with that bondage again! Do not go back! Move forward in a different direction.   Once you come into the knowledge of the truth, you cannot go back to living the way you use to live. Stop sleeping around women with all these different men. Men, stop sleeping around with all these different women. THE TERMINOLOGY IS WHOREMONGER! Do not be a fornicator or an adulterer. Some may find this shocking but **THE TRUTH WILL SET YOU FREE!** STOP FORNICATING! STOP COMMITTING ADULTERY! STOP LYING! STOP BEING SCARED AND AFRAID TO TELL PEOPLE THE TRUTH.
Embrace the truth. The saints are going to judge the angels and the world.

Do ye not know that the saints shall judge the world? And if the world shall be judged by you, are ye unworthy to judge the smallest matters?
(I Corinthians 6:2).

If you see your brother or sister sin, what are you going to do? Will you tell them the truth? Or, will you turn your back and act like you do not see what is going on? Do not go to hell for lying and sparing a person's feelings because you will be held accountable if you do not tell the truth. So if you know someone that is committing adultery, give them scriptures about adultery because they may not know the truth yet. Getting back to marriage, it is important not to lay with different people because spirits transfer. When a person fornicates, have sex with someone that they are not married to, they are taking on all those spirits of people that the person committed the act with, and then some. This means they are no longer sleeping with one person, they are sleeping with every one this person has been with in the past. The term is called "SOUL TIES." Soul ties can be defined as being linked to a spirit. There is a whole other realm out here in the universe which is called the spiritual realm.

Do not be unequally yoked with unbelievers!

When you are considering marriage, you should make sure you do not get into a relationship with or marry the wrong person. What I am saying is not to be unequally yoked with unbelievers. What does light and darkness have in common? Nothing! You will know if you are with the wrong person because you will start seeing the signs of how the individuals walk and talk does not line up with the word of God. Be very observant about this because people will often times try to deceive you every chance they get. How? By quoting certain scriptures in the bible or trying to tell you what thus said the Lord. Be very careful of who your spirit is attached and joined to. Make sure you are not one with a harlot. The two spirits are then made one. So make sure God has given you an answer about your spouse.

> *For this cause shall a man leave his father and mother, and cleave to his wife; And they twain shall be one flesh: so then they are no more twain but one flesh. What therefore God hath joined together, let no man put asunder* (Mark 10:7-9).

How does a man know how to be a good husband if he has no direction from God? How does he understand his responsibilities as a husband that he must give unto his wife? How will a woman know how to be a good wife if she has not spent some time with God? Here are several examples to follow if you are considering marriage.

Marriage Scriptures

NOW concerning the things whereof ye wrote unto me: It is good for a man not to touch a woman. Nevertheless, to avoid fornication, let every man have his own wife, and let every woman have her own husband. Let the husband render unto the wife due benevolence: and likewise also the wife unto the husband. The wife hath not power of her own body, but the husband: and likewise also the husband hath not power of his own body, but the wife. Defraud ye not one the other, except it be with consent for a time, that ye may give yourselves to fasting and prayer; and come together again, that Satan tempt you not for your incontinency (I Corinthians 7:1-5).

Wives, submit yourselves unto your own husbands, as unto the Lord. For the husband is the head of the wife, even as Christ is the head of the church: and he is the saviour of the body. Therefore as the church is subject unto Christ, so let the wives be to their own husbands in every thing. Husbands, love your wives, even as Christ also loved the church, and gave himself for it; That he might sanctify and cleanse it with the washing of water by the word, That he might present it to himself a glorious church, not having spot, or wrinkle, or any such thing; but that it should be holy and without blemish. So ought men to love their wives as their own bodies. He that loveth his wife loveth himself. For no man ever yet hated his own flesh; but nourisheth and cherisheth it, even as the Lord the church: For we are members of his body, of his flesh, and of his bones. For this cause shall a man leave his father and mother, and shall be joined unto his wife, and they two shall be one flesh. This is a great mystery: but I speak concerning Christ and the church. Nevertheless let every one of you in particular so love his wife even as himself; and the wife see that she reverence her husband (Ephesians 5:22-33).

*Wives, submit yourselves unto your own husbands,
as it is fit in the Lord. Husbands, love your wives,
and be not bitter against them* (Colossians 3:18-19).

PRAYER TO GET YOUR DELIVERANCE FROM ANYTHING THAT HAS YOU IN BONDAGE

Lord, let the anointing manifest, deliver and set me free from any uncleanness and sin in my life, whether it is spiritual ties, seducing spirits, familiar spirits, alcoholism, drugs, smoking, fornication, adultery, lust, lying, pornography, unfaithfulness, lasciviousness or witchcraft, I rebuke all these unclean spirits in the name of Jesus. I cast these spirits to the very bottom of the pit of hell where they will no longer rule my mortal body. In Jesus name I apply the blood of Jesus! Thank you Lord that I am delivered from whatever strongholds that have me in bondage in Jesus name. Let the anointing power of your precious Holy Ghost rest over my life in the name of Jesus I call it done!

STOP LOOKING FOR LOVE IN ALL THE WRONG PLACES AND LOOK TO GOD

Many people are looking for love in all the wrong places. All you have to do is look to God. If at first you learn how to love God, then yourself, just maybe it will not be so hard for you to love others. Being whole and complete with God is the first step of understanding how to express true love. True love is something that takes time to develop. When you reach this point you will have the love of God inside.

> *Beloved, let us love one another: for love is of God; and every one that loveth is born of God, and knoweth God. He that loveth not knoweth not God; for God is love. In this was manifested the love of God toward us, because that God sent his only begotten Son into the world, that we might live through him. Herein is love, not that we loved God, but that he loved us, and sent his Son to be the propitiation for our sins. Beloved, if God so loved us, we ought also to love one another*
> (I John 4:7-11).

KEEP YOUR MOUTH OFF PEOPLE, THIS IS A FORM OF WITCHCRAFT

Once you come into the knowledge of the truth, you must learn to keep your mouth off other people. Stop killing people with your tongue! Remember that you are talking about God, if you are talking about others. God made everything in the earth. The God in you is what most people fail to see. How else do you think God can come into the world, there must be a willing vessel of righteousness. God is the only one that can destroy both body and soul. There is only one that has a heaven or a hell to put you in and that is "God!"

> *But the tongue can no man tame; it is an unruly*
> *evil, full of deadly poison. Therewith bless we God,*
> *even the Father; and therewith curse we men, which*
> *are made after the similitude of God. Out of the*
> *same mouth proceedeth blessing and cursing. My*
> *brethren , these things ought not so to be. Doth a*
> *fountain send forth at the same place sweet water*
> *and bitter? Can the fig tree, my brethren, bear olive*
> *berries? Either a vine, figs? so can no fountain both*
> *yield salt water and fresh.* (James 3:8-12).

Stay Around Positive People, Let the Negative People Go!
It is important for everyone to have the spirit of discernment in order to find out the different type of spirit a person has inside them. Being surrounded by positive people is important to do once you become saved. One

thing have I learned is that in order to succeed or get any where in life an individual should have a positive attitude. As you all know, God has the final say so over your life. Before the foundation of the world, your path is already in place along with the boundaries of what you can and cannot do in life. This means you have an important part to play in controlling your own destiny by being either a positive or negative individual. It is your decision to choose the road you travel in life. The right path or the wrong path. If you live your life for God by walking the straight and narrow, then you will be on the right track.

A VIRTUOUS WOMAN OF GOD

Who can find a virtuous? for her price is far above rubies (Proverbs 31:10).

What does it mean to be a virtuous woman of God? A virtuous woman of God, is a woman who fears the Lord, loves her husband and able to take care of her household. No matter what, she must fear the Lord. In fearing the Lord, she will keep her virtue!

A virtuous woman is a crown to her husband: but she that maketh ashamed is as rottenness in his bones (Proverbs 12:4).

Neither was the man created for the woman; but the woman for the man. For this cause ought the woman to have power on her head because of the angels. Nevertheless neither is the man without the woman, neither the woman without the man, in the Lord (I Corinthians 11:9-11).

In like manner also, that women adorn themselves in modest apparel, with shamefacedness and sobriety; not with broided hair, or gold, or pearls, or costly array; But which becometh women professing godliness with good works (I Timothy 2:9-10).

How to become a virtuous woman of God

1. Value your body and obey the Holy Ghost.
2. Consecrate yourself by fasting and praying.
3. Do not have sex until you are married to your own husband!

CHAPTER 6

CLOSING THE DOOR TO YOUR PAST

Whom God hath set forth to be a propitiation through faith in his blood, to declare his righteousness for the remission of sins that are past, through the forbearance of God (Romans 3:25);

CLOSING THE DOOR TO YOUR PAST FOR GOOD!

Close the door! Slam it! Shut it! Do not think twice about looking back! If you evaluate every relationship that did not work out or last, you will begin to rejoice, jump and shout instead of digressing and trying to go back and re-kindle the fire in a relationship that just was not meant to be. If it is hard to get over someone, maybe there is a "familiar spirit" still present. It may be a "seducing spirit", a "lying spirit", or a "fornicating spirit". It is some type of spirit that is common between the two individuals, or maybe it is a generational curse. A generational curse is a pattern, a cycle that is continually passed down from generation to generation through your genes or from personality characteristics. Imagine back in the day when you first started dating, who did you date? And why did you date the person? What attracted you to them? What brought the distance in the relationship? What caused the relationship to fail? Getting back to who did you date. Did you date the person because of looks, compatibility, or just because you wanted to experiment? Whatever the reason, this is what started the very first trend and cycle of the kind of people attracted to you. From this point on, whatever type of spirit this individual had, you had to have it as well.

Nevertheless, to avoid fornication, let every man have his own wife, and let every woman have her own husband (I Corinthians 7:2).

How hard is it to obey the word of God? Not hard at all if you just apply the commandments to your life by eating your own words. So this analogy is the same as breaking the cycle and the generation curse of fornication and this is done by sanctifying your body by abstaining from fleshly lusts. Through faith all things are possible to them that believe.

NOW faith is the substance of things hoped for, the evidence of things not seen (Hebrews 11:1).

Break the spirit by: first acknowledging what kind of spirit it is and rebuke it in the name of Jesus. Then apply to your life what is said in I Corinthians 6:9-20 and saturate your spirit with the word of God. Second, you are a product of what you receive in your spirit and what you hear. Third, read the word daily.

Know ye not that ye are the temple of God, and that the Spirit of God dwelleth in you If any man defile

the temple of God, him shall God destroy; for the
temple of God is holy, which temple ye are
(I Corinthians 3:16-17).

This is real and if you really truly believe totally by releasing your faith in God, then you will abide in his word and obey God. When you serve God, you either have to serve him whole heartily or not serve him at all. Do not be lukewarm. Are you a worshipper of God or a doubter that is gone astray? Remember to worship God in spirit and in truth. It is impossible to really serve God freely to the fullest extent if you are still in your sins. Therefore, it is impossible to be in the flesh and understand the things of the spirit and it is impossible to be spiritually and continue in sin. When you become dead to sin, then you will receive a revelation from God. God will start speaking. In order to hear from God you must be keen to his Spirit and able to know how to hear the voice of God.

But the natural man receiveth not the things of the
Spirit of God: for they are foolishness unto him:
neither can he know them, because they are
spiritually discerned. But he that is spiritual
judgeth all things, yet he himself is judged of no

man. For who hath known the mind of the Lord, that he may instruct him? But we have the mind of Christ (I Corinthians 2:14-16).

And you hath he quickened who were dead in trespasses and sins; (Ephesians 2:1).

CHAPTER 7

THE HOLY SPIRIT

Which things also we speak, not in the words which man's wisdom teacheth, but which the Holy Ghost teacheth; comparing spiritual things with spiritual (I Corinthians 2:13).

THE HOLY SPIRIT

The Holy Spirit is the inner voice you hear that will lead, guide and convict. If a person has the Holy Spirit, which is the Spirit of God, then he/she is of God. God does not want you to perish. The Holy Spirit is a gentlemen, he will not force himself on you. The Holy Spirit is also known as "The Comforter". In order to receive, you must believe in your heart that he is God.

> *Then Peter said unto them, Repent, and be baptized every one of you in the name of Jesus Christ for the remission of sins, and ye shall receive the gift of the Holy Ghost* (Acts 2:38).

I remember when I was young and in church I use to see people run around the church screaming, shouting and dancing. I always wondered if this was having the Holy Ghost. If so, then why would so many still do the same thing as the world, like going to night clubs, drinking, cussing, and talking about others. I mean come on this surely is not having the Holy Ghost, "I pondered". As I had began to study the word of God more, I found out that the Holy Ghost is the Comforter. The Holy Ghost is power and in order to receive it you must be in extreme obedience to God.

> *John answered, saying unto them all, I indeed baptize you with water; but one mightier than I cometh, the latchet of whose shoes I am not worthy to unloose: he shall baptize you with the Holy Ghost and with fire* (Luke 3:16):

> *And the Holy Ghost descended in a bodily shape like a dove upon him, and a voice came from heaven, which said, Thou art my beloved Son; in thee I am well pleased* (Luke 3:22).

Now you should understand exactly what the Holy Ghost is and how to receive the gift. Do not be surprised if you have to tarry until it comes, but remember it will come just be obedient to the word of God.

The (9) Gifts of the Spirit are: word of wisdom, word of knowledge, faith, gifts of healing, working of miracles, prophecy, discerning of spirits, divers kinds of tongues and interpretation of tongues.

JESUS IS THE ANSWER

If you say that you believe in God then you must have faith.

> *For a just man falleth seven times, and riseth up*
> *again: But the wicked shall fall into mischief*
> (Proverbs 24:16).

It is evident that you have to come to Jesus just the way you are with everything that has you in bondage. Jesus is ready and willing to receive you no matter what you have done, no matter how many times you have done it. Jesus is waiting on you to come to him and give all your problems to him. The Lord can solve them all and he is waiting to accept you with open arms. Jesus will forgive you! I am a living witness. If you do not believe, just try Jesus and get to know him on your own. God is using you to be a witness to his people in the earth. If you confess with your mouth and make your requests known to God, anything you ask without doubting, God will give it to you. The key here is that you must believe in your heart and speak positive things into your life and God will manifest. God is not a liar, there is no lie or uncleanness in him.

Now unto him that is able to do exceeding
abundantly above all that we ask or think,
according to the power that worketh in us. Unto him
be glory in the church by Christ Jesus throughout
all ages, world without end (Ephesians 3:20).

Everything you need from God is given to you according to his word. To break it down, you must read the bible, believe in your heart every word of the bible, and have faith in God.

FOR AS MUCH then as Christ hath suffered for us
in the flesh, arm yourselves likewise with the same
mind: for he that hath suffered in the flesh hath
ceased from sin; That he no longer should live the
rest of his time in the flesh to the lusts of men but to
the will of God (I Peter 4:1-2).

Know that in life there will always be tests and trials and you have to pass each test in order to proceed to the next level in life. This is called the trying of your faith. The tests come in life so that you can move further and get to the next step towards your destiny in life that is purposed by God. Trust in the Lord! If you are going to pray, then why do you worry? Prove yourself to God by totally submitting to him in faith. When you speak words out loud, you are bringing life to your situation by shaping what you say into existence. Try it and the manifestation shall take place in your life.

> *Every word of God is pure: he is a shield unto them that put their trust in him* (Proverbs 30:5).

> *Iron sharpeneth iron; so a man sharpeneth the countenance of his friend* (Proverbs 27:17).

Why Not Just Believe God For Everything. What Do You Have To Lose?

Oftentimes people are in denial about themselves or about the things they continue to do in life that is not pleasing in the sight of God. Life is all about making choices and sometimes you make good choices and other times you make bad choices. So, whether you make the decision to believe in God or not it is totally your choice.

Stay positive and have faith in God and know he will work everything out for your good. If it is lack of faith, then start thanking God for faith. God is Jehovah Jireh, My Provider, he will supply all of your needs. God is Jehovah Rapha,

The Lord that Heals. He can heal a broken heart, he can heal you from all your sickness and diseases if you believe in your heart and know that he is a healer. God is Jehovah Shalom, The Lord God of Peace. If you would only cast your cares upon him and leave them with him he will keep you in perfect peace, whose mind is stayed on thee. If you would only believe and thank God for being Jehovah Shammah because "he is with you". God will never leave or forsake you because his Spirit is with you and in you. Do you really believe that God is Jehovah Tsidkenu, The Lord God my Righteousness? He is! He is God who forgives you and the God who helps you forgive and love unconditionally.

CHAPTER 8

WHAT HAPPEN TO THE TRUTH?

Study to shew thyself approved unto God, a workman that needeth not to be ashamed, rightly dividing the word of truth (II Timothy 2:15).

Brethren, if any of you do err from the truth, and one convert him; Let him know, that he which converteth the sinner from the error of his way, shall save a soul from death, and shall hide a multitude of sins (James 5 19-20).

What Is The Position Of the Church?

> *Take heed therefore unto yourselves, and to all the flock, over the which the Holy Ghost hath made you overseers, to feed the church of God, which he hath purchased with his own blood. For I know this, that after my departing shall grievous wolves enter in among you, not sparing the flock* (Acts 20:28-29).

There is a need for unity within the church because there are too many people in the church that are not sure if they are really saved, which means that their souls are in the balance. If you cannot answer the question, If you died today do you know for sure that you would go to heaven? If your answer is anything other than yes, then there is a problem, because you do not know where you will spend eternity. You must know what the word of God says about salvation. Salvation is to know for sure that you are saved without a doubt in your mind. There is no guessing about it!

Speaking on Salvation

When you receive salvation (accept Jesus Christ) you must repent and turn from your wicked ways, be baptized in Jesus name and you shall receive the gift of the Holy Ghost.

1. Repentance, Acts 2:38, II Timothy 2:25-26 (Study and know the word for yourself).
   In meekness instructing those that oppose themselves; if God peradventure will give them repentance to the acknowledging of the truth; And that they may recover themselves out of the snare of the devil, who are taken captive by him at his will (II Timothy 2:25-26).

2. Baptism, Acts 2:38-39, John 3:3-7, I John 5:6-8.
   Then Peter said unto them, Repent, and be baptized every one of you in the name of Jesus Christ for the remission of sins, and ye shall receive the gift of the Holy Ghost. For the promise is unto you, and to your children, and to all that are afar off, even as many as the Lord our God shall call (Acts 2:38-39).

This is he that came by water and blood, even Jesus Christ; not by water only, but by water and blood. And it is the Spirit that beareth witness, because the Spirit is truth. For there are three that bear record in heaven, the Father, the Word, and the Holy Ghost: and these three are one. And there are three that bear witness in earth, the Spirit, and the water, and the blood: and these three agree in one
(I John 5:6-8).

3. The Holy Ghost, I Corinthians 12:7-11.

Many believers' lifestyles are not lining up with what the word of God says. If a life changing word is being preached, that is the truth, **THEN MORE DELIVERANCE WOULD TAKE PLACE IN THE CHURCH TODAY AND THE PEOPLE WOULD NOT BE ABLE TO LEAVE THE CHURCH THE SAME WAY THEY CAME IN.** People would actually be convicted by the Holy Spirit to turn from their evil ways and then be able to obey the word of God. It is the anointing that destroys the yolk.

And it shall come to pass in that day, that his
burden shall be taken away from off thy shoulder,
and his yolk from off thy neck, and the yoke shall be
destroyed because of the anointing (Isaiah 10:27).

What is really going on in the church? Where is God's chosen in the church? Where are all the anointed men and women of God? Are the anointed in their right position in the church? If not, then God will soon place the anointed in their rightful position. Or is it because very few are practicing what they preach? If this is the case, God will expose it. Be careful not to prostitute the gift of the Holy Ghost!

But the anointing which ye have received of him
abideth in you, and ye need not that any man teach
you: but as the same anointing teacheth you of all
things, and is truth, and is no lie, and even as it
hath taught you, ye shall abide in him (I John 2:27).

Touch not mine anointed, and do my prophets no
harm (Psalms 105:15).

115

I hope this revelation helps someone get into position. There is a hurting and dying generation that is lost. To all churches, I ask you, What are you going to do about it? Will many churches step up to the plate and preach the TRUTH? What about the harvest? The church has a lot of work to do.

> *Therefore said he unto them, The harvest truly is great, but the labourers are few: pray ye therefore the Lord of the harvest, that he would send forth labourers into his harvest* (Luke 10:2).

There are many people who do not belong to a church and want to change and they are seeking the truth but cannot find it. It is time for the church to get in order and get on one accord. If God said it in his word it shall come to pass. Judgment must begin at the house of God!

The Purpose of The Church

Jesus Christ is the head of the church. The main purpose of the "church" is for all believers to assemble and worship God with other believers. The church comprises of two types: the saved and the unsaved. Which also can be defined again as the righteous (the godly) and the unrighteous (the ungodly). So, if you have those who are saved and unsaved in the church, then the saved should pray and intercede for the unsaved. The strong ought to bear the infirmities of the weak. Not everybody in church is saved. Remember now, when God came, the devil came also. The spirit of manipulation is running rapid in the churches today. It is time out for being all about money!

> *There is one body, and one Spirit, even as ye are called in one hope of your calling; One Lord, on faith, one baptism, One God and Father of all, who is above all, and through all, and in you all. But unto every one of us is given grace according to the measure of the gift of Christ.* (Ephesians 4:4-7).

> *That we henceforth be no more children, tossed to and fro, and carried about with every wind of doctrine by the sleight of men, and cunning craftiness, whereby they lie in wait to deceive. But speaking the truth in love, may grow up in him in all things, which is the head, even Christ:* (Ephesians 4:14-15). **Ephesians 4:16-27, Read it for yourself.**

The church, which is comprised of believers' responsibility is to help win souls for Christ, not to condemn people but to meet the people at the point of their need just as Jesus Christ did. If you believe what the Bible says then you can do it. Do not just pick out and choose what you will obey and what you will not obey, because you must obey everything that the word of God says. God will expose you and pull back the cover if you are living a lie. Get it together! Do not just go to church on Sunday, it does not end there. It is an everyday mission to walk the walk and talk the talk. If you have a calling or a ministry, then it is an everyday mission and your life must be in line with the word of God in order for breakthroughs to occur in the lives of others under your Ministry. When you are behind closed doors remember if no one else can see you that God can see everything. God knows exactly who you are. So just remember that they that worship God must worship God in spirit and in truth.

What Happen To The Truth?

> *But the hour cometh, and now is, when the true worshippers shall worship the Father in spirit and in truth: for the Father seeketh such to worship*

him. God is a Spirit: and they that worship him
must worship him in spirit and in truth
(John 4:23-24).

What happen to obedience and judgment. It seems as if all that is being taught now is just all about blessings and prosperity. **THIS IS GREAT! BUT IN ORDER TO EXPERIENCE BLESSINGS AND PROSPERITY, YOU MUST OBEY THE WORD OF GOD FIRST BECAUSE GOD IS NOT GOING TO BLESS YOU IF YOU ARE NOT KEEPING HIS COMMANDMENTS!** In Malachi 3:8-1, the scriptures talk about offering. Therefore, if anyone is being manipulated in giving, ask God to open your eyes!

If we say that we have fellowship with him, and
walk in darkness, we lie, and do not the truth: But
if we walk in the light, as he is in the light, we have
fellowship one with another, and the blood of Jesus
Christ his Son cleanseth us from all sin
(I John 1:6-7).

And hereby we do know that we know him, if we
keep his commandments. He that saith, I know him,

and keepeth not his commandments, is a liar, and the truth is not in him (I John 2:3-4).

It is time for all churches to get in line according to the word of God. If you are not being taught "**sound doctrine**", understand that any other kind of doctrine is not of God. Beware of the doctrines of devils. Do not be deceived by false prophets. I advise you to study the bible and seek wisdom from above because there is too much manipulation, witchcraft and trickery going on in the house of God today.

> *For the time is come that judgment must begin at the house of God: and if it first begin at us, what shall the end be of them that obey not the gospel of God? And if the righteous scarcely be saved, where shall the ungodly and the sinner appear?* (I Peter 4:17-18).

This is the truth. Embrace the truth and get set free today. God is watching! So make sure you are practicing what you preach? Note: God has no respect of persons! (Colossians 3:25).

CHAPTER 9

ANYONE WITH AN ADDICTION

Your iniquities have turned away these things, and your sins have witholden good things from you (Jeremiah 5:25).

To Anyone with an Addiction

What? know ye not that your body is the temple of the Holy Ghost which is in you, which ye have of God, and ye are not your own? (I Corinthians 6:19).

Can you please take care of your body! I conducted my own self-study with individuals that smoke, drink alcohol and use drugs and I found out they are looking for a way of escape from their responsibilities in life. Individuals are looking for alternative ways to keep their mind off their problems. But the truth of the matter is that once they come off of their high, they come to their senses and all the same problems and issues are still there. News flash, the problems and issues will not go away until the individuals get their mind right. God can solve your problems, if you give them to him. Now you are still stuck in the same situation. What do you do? I am going to give you some ways to get free. It is then totally up to you to follow the steps.

Step 1: Stop being in denial and embrace the truth that you have an addiction.

Step 2: Admit that you are addicted to smoking,

alcohol, or drugs, or anything that has you in bondage.

Step 3: Accept the help that is being offered.
Ask God to help you quit and mean it from your heart!

Step 4: Realize the fact that you can have major health problems that can and will cause death. Such as strokes and heart attacks from drugs; lung cancer and other types of cancer causing symptoms from smoking, liver disease, and kidney failure and other diseases from drinking alcohol.

Step 5: Pray and ask God for deliverance from the substance abuse additions and be sincere and willing to give an honest effort to change. Get help and go to drug and alcohol treatment facilities that offer support to help you quit!

Step 6: Change your environment and thinking. Start hanging around people that are not addicted to drugs and alcohol and stay positive and do not get hooked back on these substances again.

Step 7: Read the bible daily.
Know that God loves you and cares so much about you! Get saved and stay saved!

Meditate on the following scriptures that will help you get set free.

What? know ye not that your body is the temple of the Holy Ghost which is in you, which ye have of God, and ye are not your own? For ye are bought with a price: therefore glorify God in your body, and in your spirit, which are God's (I Corinthians 6:19-20).

And what agreement hath the temple of God with idols? for ye are the temple of the living God; as God hath said, I will dwell in them, and walk in them; and I will be their God, and they shall be my people. Wherefore come out from among them, and be ye separate, saith the Lord, and touch not the unclean thing; and I will receive you, And will be a Father unto you, and ye shall be my sons and daughters, saith the Lord Almighty (II Corinthians 6:16-18).

Knowing this, that our old man is crucified with him, that the body of sin might be destroyed, that henceforth we should not serve sin (Romans 6:6).

I BESEECH you therefore, brethren, by the mercies of God, that ye present your bodies a living sacrifice, holy, acceptable unto God, which is your reasonable service (Romans 12:1).

HOW TO GET SAVED

1. Repent and turn from evil.
2. Be baptized in the Name of Jesus.
3. You shall receive the gift of the Holy Ghost.

Scriptures to study regarding "salvation"

II Corinthians 7:10, repentance to salvation
Philippians 1:19, this shall turn to my salvation
Romans 10:10, confession is made to salvation
Acts 4:12, neither is there salvation in any other
II Peter 3:15, longsuffering of the Lord is salvation
Hebrews 1:14, for them who shall be heirs of salvation
Ephesians 1:13, the gospel of your salvation
Romans 1:16, the power of God unto salvation
II Corinthians 1:6, comforted, it is for your salvation
Titus 2:11, grace of God that bringeth salvation
Romans 13:11, now is our salvation nearer
Luke 3:6, all flesh shall see the salvation of God
Acts 13:26, to you is the word of salvation sent
I Thessalonians 5:9, hath appointed us to obtain salvation

Deliverance from Alcohol Addiction Prayer

I thank you Jesus for caring so much about me by giving me another chance to get my life together for you. Lord, Jesus I am a believer and not a doubter and I know that greater is he that is in me than he that is in the world! Thank you Jesus for life and peace of mind. I rebuke the **Alcohol Addiction** that I have right now in the name of Jesus. God I recognize and know that my problems will not go away until I totally submit and give my life to you. Today, I lay my burdens down and give them to you. I am now set free and no longer held captive by the powers of darkness. I thank you God that you love me so much that you will never leave me nor forsake me. In Jesus name I seal it with the Blood of Jesus. Now I am able to seek you first and follow the plan that you have set for my life. I love you God and I thank you in Jesus name I am free!

Deliverance from Drug Addiction Prayer

I thank you Jesus for caring so much about me by giving me another chance to get my life together for you. Lord, Jesus I am a believer and not a doubter and I know that greater is he that is in me than he that is in the world! Thank you Jesus for life and peace of mind. I rebuke the **Drug Addiction** that I have right now in the name of Jesus. God I recognize and know that my problems will not go away until I totally submit and give my life to you. Today, I lay my burdens down and give them to you. I am now set free and no longer held captive by the powers of darkness. I thank you God that you love me so much that you will never leave me nor forsake me. In Jesus name I seal it with the Blood of Jesus. Now I am able to seek you first and follow the plan that you have set for my life. I love you God and I thank you in Jesus name I am free!

Deliverance from Smoking Addiction Prayer

I thank you Jesus for caring so much about me by giving me another chance to get my life together for you. Lord, Jesus I am a believer and not a doubter and I know that greater is he that is in me than he that is in the world! Thank you Jesus for life and peace of mind. I rebuke the **Smoking Addiction** that I have right now in the name of Jesus. God I recognize and know that my problems will not go away until I totally submit and give my life to you. Today, I lay my burdens down and give them to you. I am now set free and no longer held captive by the powers of darkness. I thank you God that you love me so much that you will never leave me nor forsake me. In Jesus name I seal it with the Blood of Jesus. Now I am able to seek you first and follow the plan that you have set for my life. I love you God and I thank you in Jesus name I am free!

ARE YOU A WATCHMAN?

A watchman is someone that is sent out to warn the people of God from the evil. The individual is someone God can trust to deliver the message directly to the people with boldness exactly how it should be delivered. This means that there is not going to be any sugar coating the word of God.

> *AGAIN the word of the LORD came unto me, saying, Son of man, speak to the children of thy people, and say unto them, When I bring the sword upon a land, if the people of the land take a man of their coasts, and set him for their watchman: If when he seeth the sword come upon the land, he blow the trumpet, and warn the people;*
> *Then whosoever heareth the sound of the trumpet, and taketh not warning; if the sword come, and take him away, his blood shall be upon his own head. He heard the sound of the trumpet, and took not warning; his blood shall be upon him. But he that taketh warning shall deliver his soul.*
> *But if the watchman see the sword come, and blow not the trumpet, and the people be not warned; if the sword come, and take any person from among*

them, he is taken away in his iniquity; but his blood will I require at the watchman's hand. So thou, O son of man, I have set thee a watchman unto the house of Israel; therefore thou shalt hear the word at my mouth, and warn them from me. When I say unto the wicked, O wicked man, thou shalt surely die; if thou dost not speak to warn the wicked from his way, that wicked man shall die in his iniquity; but his blood will I require at thine hand. Nevertheless, if thou warn the wicked of his way to turn from it; if he do not turn from his way, he shall die in his iniquity; but thou hast delivered thy soul (Ezekiel 33:1-9).

God is going to hold you accountable if you do not tell people the truth.

CRY aloud, spare not, lift up thy voice like a trumpet, and shew my people their transgression, and the house of Jacob their sins (Isaiah 58:1).

Tell the people about their sins because if they are believers and not obeying Gods word then their blessings are going to miss them.

His watchmen are blind: they are all ignorant, they are all dumb dogs, they cannot bark; sleeping, lying down, loving to slumber (Isaiah 56:10).

Let us not be like the dumb dogs that cannot bark. Tell people the truth about their sins and if they do not want to change and turn from their ways, then you have completed your task because their blood will not be on your hands. It is then totally up to that individual to desire to change and God will deal with them. There are many that ran and have not been called, so how can one preach the gospel if they were not chosen by God. The key here is that the anointing is going to determine whether or not someone is chosen and sent verses rather or not they ran and called themselves. Think about it. In order for the word of God to go forth with deliverance power and set the captives free, one must be chosen by God and "anointed" to preach the gospel!

CHAPTER 10

HOW TO BREAK GENERATIONAL CURSES

Thou shalt not bow down thyself unto them, nor serve them: for I the Lord thy God am a jealous God, visiting the iniquity of the fathers upon the children unto the third and fourth generation of them that hate me, And shewing mercy unto thousands of them that love me and keep my commandments (Deuteronomy 5:9-10).

How to Break the Generational Curses

What are generational curses? Generational curses are traits that we passed on from one generation to another generation. For example, if a relative is an alcoholics or drug abuser, then chances are their children will have the same problem. This is a cycle that must be stopped. In order to break Generational Curses, you must obey the word of God period. The cycle can stop once you repent and be baptized in the name of Jesus. To break generational curses, it is important that you have a personal relationship with Jesus Christ that is consistent. The generational curses can be broken by being born again. The key is to believe and get baptized in Jesus name and know that you are covered by the blood of Jesus in order to have power over the devil.

1. **You must first walk in obedience, repent, be baptized in the name of Jesus and ye shall receive the gift of the Holy Ghost.**

Whatever the generational curse is in your family call it out and put it under the blood of Jesus and walk in extreme obedience unto God. In order to worship God you must obey the commandments of God.

2. Use the Name of Jesus when you pray because there is power in the name of Jesus!

And the seventy returned again with joy, saying, Lord, even the devils are subject unto us through thy name. And he said unto them, I beheld Satan as lighting fall from heaven. Behold, I give unto you power to tread on serpents and scorpions, and over all the power of the enemy: and nothing shall by any means hurt you (Luke 10:17-19).

So that from his body were brought unto the sick handkerchiefs or aprons, and the diseases departed from them, and the evil spirits went out of them. Then certain of the vagabond Jews, exorcists, took upon them to call over them which had evil spirits the name of the Lord Jesus saying, We adjure you by Jesus whom Paul preacheth. And there were seven sons of one Sce'-va, a Jew, and chief of the priests, which did so. And the evil spirit answered and said, Jesus I know, and Paul I know; but who are ye? And the man in whom the evil spirit was leaped on them, and overcame them, and prevailed

against them, so that they fled out of that house
naked and wounded. And this was known to all the
Jews and Greeks also dwelling at Eph'-e-sus; and
fear fell on them all, and the name of the Lord Jesus
was magnified. And many that believed came, and
confessed, and shewed their deeds. Many of them
also which used curious arts brought their books
together, and burned them before all men: and they
counted the price of them, and found it fifty
thousand pieces of silver (Acts 19:12-19).

The seal is the Blood of Jesus!

And he called them unto him, and said unto them in
parables, How can Satan cast out Satan? And if a
kingdom be divided against itself, that kingdom
cannot stand. And if a house be divided against
itself, that house cannot stand. And if Satan rise up
against himself, and be divided, he cannot stand,
but hath an end. No man can enter into a strong
man's house, and spoil his goods, except he will
first bind the strong man; and then he will spoil his
house (Mark 3:23-27).

3. **Seal it with the blood of Jesus.** The seal is when you receive the gift of the Holy Ghost once you get baptized in Jesus name.

In whom ye also trusted, after that ye heard the word of truth, the gospel of your salvation: in whom also after that ye believed, ye were sealed with that Holy Spirit of promise
(Ephesians 1:13).
How much more shall the blood of Christ, who through the eternal Spirit offered himself without spot to God, purge your conscience from dead works to serve the living God?
(Hebrews 9:14).

To break the curses you must be baptized in the name of Jesus and have already received the gift of the Holy Ghost.

He that believeth and is baptized shall be saved; but he that believeth not shall be damned. And these signs shall follow them that believe; In my name shall they cast out devils; they shall speak with new tongues; They shall take up serpents; and if they drink any deadly thing, it shall not hurt them; they

shall lay hands on the sick, and they shall recover
(Mark 16:16-18).

The devil is always trying to deceive the children of God and throw you off course by reminding you to look back and reflect on your past. In order to overcome, you have to come to the realization and know that God is ordering your steps. Then it is totally up to you if you continue thinking about your past, or look back. Look to God because he has so much for you once you decide to obey word.   When you make the decision, then seal it with the Blood of Jesus! **PUT IT ALL UNDER THE BLOOD OF JESUS!** Do not look back. Always remember to submit yourselves therefore to God, resist the devil and he will flee from you Read more in James chapter 4.

CHAPTER 11

THE CHARGE TO BREAK GENERATIONAL CURSES

When Jesus saw that the people came running together, he rebuked the foul spirit, saying unto him, Thou dumb and deaf spirit, I charge thee, come out of him, and enter no more into him (Mark 9:25)

And he said unto them, This kind can come forth by nothing, but by prayer and fasting (Mark 9:29)

The Charge To Break The Generational Curse of
UNBELIEF

Jesus, I break the generational curse of UNBELIEF that has me in bondage and any other generational curses that happened in my family with and without my knowledge of it happening. I rebuke all these curses in the name of Jesus! Lord I am a servant of you and obedient to your holy word and I know that your word cannot come back to you void. So, I believe in my heart that all of the curses of **unbelief** are now broken in my life and in my family's life. The curses of **unbelief** are broken off of my children and their children's children. I repent God of all my sins and I put it all under the blood. In the name of Jesus I rebuke the generational curse of **unbelief** and **I charge** the spirit of **unbelief** to come out of me, and enter no more into me in the name of Jesus. It is done!

And he said unto them, This kind can come forth by nothing, but by prayer and fasting (Mark 9:29)

The Charge To Break The Generational Curse of
POVERTY

Jesus, I break the generational curse of POVERTY that has me in bondage and any other generational curses that happened in my family with and without my knowledge of it happening. I rebuke all these curses in the name of Jesus! Lord I am a servant of you and obedient to your holy word and I know that your word cannot come back to you void. So, I believe in my heart that all of the curses of **poverty** are now broken in my life and in my family's life. The curses of **poverty** are broken off of my children and their children's children. I repent God of all my sins and I put it all under the blood. In the name of Jesus I rebuke the generational curse of **poverty** and **I charge** the spirit of **poverty** to come out of me, and enter no more into me in the name of Jesus. It is done!

And he said unto them, This kind can come forth by nothing, but by prayer and fasting (Mark 9:29)

The Charge To Break The Generational Curse of
RAPE

Jesus, I break the generational curse of RAPE that has me in bondage and any other generational curses that happened in my family with and without my knowledge of it happening. I rebuke all these curses in the name of Jesus! Lord I am a servant of you and obedient to your holy word and I know that your word cannot come back to you void. So, I believe in my heart that all of the curses of **rape** are now broken in my life and in my family's life. The curses of **rape** are broken off of my children and their children's children. I repent God of all my sins and I put it all under the blood. In the name of Jesus I rebuke the generational curse of **rape** and **I charge** the spirit of **rape** to come out of me, and enter no more into me in the name of Jesus. It is done!

And he said unto them, This kind can come forth by nothing, but by prayer and fasting (Mark 9:29)

The Charge To Break The Generational Curse of
INCEST

Jesus, I break the generational curse of INCEST that has me in bondage and any other generational curses that happened in my family with and without my knowledge of it happening. I rebuke all these curses in the name of Jesus! Lord I am a servant of you and obedient to your holy word and I know that your word cannot come back to you void. So, I believe in my heart that all of the curses of **incest** are now broken in my life and in my family's life. The curses of **incest** are broken off of my children and their children's children. I repent God of all my sins and I put it all under the blood. In the name of Jesus I rebuke the generational curse of **incest** and **I charge** the spirit of **incest** to come out of me, and enter no more into me in the name of Jesus. It is done!

And he said unto them, This kind can come forth by nothing, but by prayer and fasting (Mark 9:29)

The Charge To Break The Generational Curse of
SEXUAL PERVERSION

Jesus, I break the generational curse of SEXUAL PERVERSION that has me in bondage and any other generational curses that happened in my family with and without my knowledge of it happening. I rebuke all these curses in the name of Jesus! Lord I am a servant of you and obedient to your holy word and I know that your word cannot come back to you void. So, I believe in my heart that all of the curses of **sexual perversion** are now broken in my life and in my family's life. The curses of **sexual perversion** are broken off of my children and their children's children. I repent God of all my sins and I put it all under the blood. In the name of Jesus I rebuke the generational curse of **sexual perversion** and **I charge** the spirit of **sexual perversion** to come out of me, and enter no more into me in the name of Jesus. It is done!

And he said unto them, This kind can come forth by nothing, but by prayer and fasting (Mark 9:29)

The Charge To Break The Generational Curse of
ALCOHOLISM

Jesus, I break the generational curse of ALCOHOLISM that has me in bondage and any other generational curses that happened in my family with and without my knowledge of it happening. I rebuke all these curses in the name of Jesus! Lord I am a servant of you and obedient to your holy word and I know that your word cannot come back to you void. So, I believe in my heart that all of the curses of **alcoholism** are now broken in my life and in my family's life. The curses of **alcoholism** are broken off of my children and their children's children. I repent God of all my sins and I put it all under the blood. In the name of Jesus I rebuke the generational curse of **alcoholism** and **I charge** the spirit of **alcoholism** to come out of me, and enter no more into me in the name of Jesus. It is done!

And he said unto them, This kind can come forth by nothing, but by prayer and fasting (Mark 9:29)

The Charge To Break The Generational Curse of
DRUG ABUSE

Jesus, I break the generational curse of DRUG ABUSE that has me in bondage and any other generational curses that happened in my family with and without my knowledge of it happening. I rebuke all these curses in the name of Jesus! Lord I am a servant of you and obedient to your holy word and I know that your word cannot come back to you void. So, I believe in my heart that all of the curses of **drug abuse** are now broken in my life and in my family's life. The curses of **drug abuse** are broken off of my children and their children's children. I repent God of all my sins and I put it all under the blood. In the name of Jesus I rebuke the generational curse of **drug abuse** and **I charge** the spirit of **drug abuse** to come out of me, and enter no more into me in the name of Jesus. It is done!

And he said unto them, This kind can come forth by nothing, but by prayer and fasting (Mark 9:29)

The Charge To Break The Generational Curse of
SMOKING

Jesus, I break the generational curse of SMOKING that has me in bondage and any other generational curses that happened in my family with and without my knowledge of it happening. I rebuke all these curses in the name of Jesus! Lord I am a servant of you and obedient to your holy word and I know that your word cannot come back to you void. So, I believe in my heart that all of the curses of **smoking** are now broken in my life and in my family's life. The curses of **smoking** are broken off of my children and their children's children. I repent God of all my sins and I put it all under the blood. In the name of Jesus I rebuke the generational curse of **smoking** and **I charge** the spirit of **smoking** to come out of me, and enter no more into me in the name of Jesus. It is done!

And he said unto them, This kind can come forth by nothing, but by prayer and fasting (Mark 9:29)

The Charge To Break The Generational Curse of
LYING

Jesus, I break the generational curse of LYING that has me in bondage and any other generational curses that happened in my family with and without my knowledge of it happening. I rebuke all these curses in the name of Jesus! Lord I am a servant of you and obedient to your holy word and I know that your word cannot come back to you void. So, I believe in my heart that all of the curses of **lying** are now broken in my life and in my family's life. The curses of **lying** are broken off of my children and their children's children. I repent God of all my sins and I put it all under the blood. In the name of Jesus I rebuke the generational curse of **lying** and **I charge** the spirit of **lying** to come out of me, and enter no more into me in the name of Jesus. It is done!

And he said unto them, This kind can come forth by nothing, but by prayer and fasting (Mark 9:29)

The Charge To Break The Generational Curse of
LOW SELF-ESTEEM

Jesus, I break the generational curse of LOW SELF-ESTEEM that has me in bondage and any other generational curses that happened in my family with and without my knowledge of it happening. I rebuke all these curses in the name of Jesus! Lord I am a servant of you and obedient to your holy word and I know that your word cannot come back to you void. So, I believe in my heart that all of the curses of **low self-esteem** are now broken in my life and in my family's life. The curses of **low self-esteem** are broken off of my children and their children's children. I repent God of all my sins and I put it all under the blood. In the name of Jesus I rebuke the generational curse of **low self-esteem** and **I charge** the spirit of **low self-esteem** to come out of me, and enter no more into me in the name of Jesus. It is done!

And he said unto them, This kind can come forth by nothing, but by prayer and fasting (Mark 9:29)

The Charge To Break The Generational Curse of
OVER EATING

Jesus, I break the generational curse of OVER EATING that has me in bondage and any other generational curses that happened in my family with and without my knowledge of it happening. I rebuke all these curses in the name of Jesus! Lord I am a servant of you and obedient to your holy word and I know that your word cannot come back to you void. So, I believe in my heart that all of the curses of **over eating** are now broken in my life and in my family's life. The curses of **over eating** are broken off of my children and their children's children. I repent God of all my sins and I put it all under the blood. In the name of Jesus I rebuke the generational curse of **over eating** and **I charge** the spirit of **over eating** to come out of me, and enter no more into me in the name of Jesus. It is done!

And he said unto them, This kind can come forth by nothing, but by prayer and fasting (Mark 9:29)

The Charge To Break The Generational Curse of
DEPRESSION

Jesus, I break the generational curse of DEPRESSION that has me in bondage and any other generational curses that happened in my family with and without my knowledge of it happening. I rebuke all these curses in the name of Jesus! Lord I am a servant of you and obedient to your holy word and I know that your word cannot come back to you void. So, I believe in my heart that all of the curses of **depression** are now broken in my life and in my family's life. The curses of **depression** are broken off of my children and their children's children. I repent God of all my sins and I put it all under the blood. In the name of Jesus I rebuke the generational curse of **depression** and **I charge** the spirit of **depression** to come out of me, and enter no more into me in the name of Jesus. It is done!

And he said unto them, This kind can come forth by nothing, but by prayer and fasting (Mark 9:29)

The Charge To Break The Generational Curse of
ADULTERY

Jesus, I break the generational curse of ADULTERY that has me in bondage and any other generational curses that happened in my family with and without my knowledge of it happening. I rebuke all these curses in the name of Jesus! Lord I am a servant of you and obedient to your holy word and I know that your word cannot come back to you void. So, I believe in my heart that all of the curses of **adultery** are now broken in my life and in my family's life. The curses of **adultery** are broken off of my children and their children's children. I repent God of all my sins and I put it all under the blood. In the name of Jesus I rebuke the generational curse of **adultery** and **I charge** the spirit of **adultery** to come out of me, and enter no more into me in the name of Jesus. It is done!

And he said unto them, This kind can come forth by nothing, but by prayer and fasting (Mark 9:29)

The Charge To Break The Generational Curse of
FORNICATION

Jesus, I break the generational curse of FORNICATION that has me in bondage and any other generational curses that happened in my family with and without my knowledge of it happening. I rebuke all these curses in the name of Jesus! Lord I am a servant of you and obedient to your holy word and I know that your word cannot come back to you void. So, I believe in my heart that all of the curses of **fornication** are now broken in my life and in my family's life. The curses of **fornication** are broken off of my children and their children's children. I repent God of all my sins and I put it all under the blood. In the name of Jesus I rebuke the generational curse of **fornication** and **I charge** the spirit of **fornication** to come out of me, and enter no more into me in the name of Jesus. It is done!

And he said unto them, This kind can come forth by nothing, but by prayer and fasting (Mark 9:29)

The Charge To Break The Generational Curse of
DIVORCE

Jesus, I break the generational curse of DIVORCE that has me in bondage and any other generational curses that happened in my family with and without my knowledge of it happening. I rebuke all these curses in the name of Jesus! Lord I am a servant of you and obedient to your holy word and I know that your word cannot come back to you void. So, I believe in my heart that all of the curses of **divorce** are now broken in my life and in my family's life. The curses of **divorce** are broken off of my children and their children's children. I repent God of all my sins and I put it all under the blood. In the name of Jesus I rebuke the generational curse of **divorce** and **I charge** the spirit of **divorce** to come out of me, and enter no more into me in the name of Jesus. It is done!

And he said unto them, This kind can come forth by nothing, but by prayer and fasting (Mark 9:29)

The Charge To Break The Generational Curse of
IMPRISONMENT

**Jesus, I break the generational curse of
IMPRISONMENT that has me in bondage and any
other generational curses that happened in my family
with and without my knowledge of it happening. I
rebuke all these curses in the name of Jesus! Lord I am
a servant of** you and obedient to your holy word and I
know that your word cannot come back to you void. So, I
believe in my heart that all of the curses of **imprisonment**
are now broken in my life and in my family's life. The
curses of **imprisonment** are broken off of my children and
their children's children. I repent God of all my sins and I
put it all under the blood. In the name of Jesus I rebuke the
generational curse of **imprisonment** and **I charge** the spirit
of **imprisonment** to come out of me, and enter no more
into me in the name of Jesus. It is done!

*And he said unto them, This kind can come forth by nothing, but by prayer and
fasting* (Mark 9:29)

The Charge To Break The Generational Curse of
SICKNESS

Jesus, I break the generational curse of SICKNESS that has me in bondage and any other generational curses that happened in my family with and without my knowledge of it happening. I rebuke all these curses in the name of Jesus! Lord I am a servant of you and obedient to your holy word and I know that your word cannot come back to you void. So, I believe in my heart that all of the curses of **sickness** are now broken in my life and in my family's life. The curses of **sickness** are broken off of my children and their children's children. I repent God of all my sins and I put it all under the blood. In the name of Jesus I rebuke the generational curse of **sickness** and **I charge** the spirit of **sickness** to come out of me, and enter no more into me in the name of Jesus. It is done!

And he said unto them, This kind can come forth by nothing, but by prayer and fasting (Mark 9:29)

The Charge To Break The Generational Curse of
DOUBT

Jesus, I break the generational curse of DOUBT that has me in bondage and any other generational curses that happened in my family with and without my knowledge of it happening. I rebuke all these curses in the name of Jesus! Lord I am a servant of you and obedient to your holy word and I know that your word cannot come back to you void. So, I believe in my heart that all of the curses of **doubt** are now broken in my life and in my family's life. The curses of **doubt** are broken off of my children and their children's children. I repent God of all my sins and I put it all under the blood. In the name of Jesus I rebuke the generational curse of **doubt** and **I charge** the spirit of **doubt** to come out of me, and enter no more into me in the name of Jesus. It is done!

And he said unto them, This kind can come forth by nothing, but by prayer and fasting (Mark 9:29)

The Charge To Break The Generational Curse of
COVETOUSNESS

Jesus, I break the generational curse of COVETOUSNESS that has me in bondage and any other generational curses that happened in my family with and without my knowledge of it happening. I rebuke all these curses in the name of Jesus! Lord I am a servant of you and obedient to your holy word and I know that your word cannot come back to you void. So, I believe in my heart that all of the curses of **covetousness** are now broken in my life and in my family's life. The curses of **covetousness** are broken off of my children and their children's children. I repent God of all my sins and I put it all under the blood. In the name of Jesus I rebuke the generational curse of **covetousness** and **I charge** the spirit of **covetousness** to come out of me, and enter no more into me in the name of Jesus. It is done!

And he said unto them, This kind can come forth by nothing, but by prayer and fasting (Mark 9:29)

The Charge To Break The Generational Curse of
MANIPULATION

Jesus, I break the generational curse of MANIPULATION that has me in bondage and any other generational curses that happened in my family with and without my knowledge of it happening. I rebuke all these curses in the name of Jesus! Lord I am a servant of you and obedient to your holy word and I know that your word cannot come back to you void. So, I believe in my heart that all of the curses of **manipulation** are now broken in my life and in my family's life. The curses of **manipulation** are broken off of my children and their children's children. I repent God of all my sins and I put it all under the blood. In the name of Jesus I rebuke the generational curse of **manipulation** and **I charge** the spirit of **manipulation** to come out of me, and enter no more into me in the name of Jesus. It is done!

And he said unto them, This kind can come forth by nothing, but by prayer and fasting (Mark 9:29)

The Charge To Break The Generational Curse of
WITCHCRAFT

Jesus, I break the generational curse of WITCHCRAFT that has me in bondage and any other generational curses that happened in my family with and without my knowledge of it happening. I rebuke all these curses in the name of Jesus! Lord I am a servant of you and obedient to your holy word and I know that your word cannot come back to you void. So, I believe in my heart that all of the curses of **witchcraft** are now broken in my life and in my family's life. The curses of **witchcraft** are broken off of my children and their children's children. I repent God of all my sins and I put it all under the blood. In the name of Jesus I rebuke the generational curse of **witchcraft** and **I charge** the spirit of **witchcraft** to come out of me, and enter no more into me in the name of Jesus. It is done!

And he said unto them, This kind can come forth by nothing, but by prayer and fasting (Mark 9:29)

The Charge To Break The Generational Curse of
HOMOSEXUALITY

Jesus, I break the generational curse of HOMOSEXUALITY that has me in bondage and any other generational curses that happened in my family with and without my knowledge of it happening. I rebuke all these curses in the name of Jesus! Lord I am a servant of you and obedient to your holy word and I know that your word cannot come back to you void. So, I believe in my heart that all of the curses of **homosexuality** are now broken in my life and in my family's life. The curses of **homosexuality** are broken off of my children and their children's children. I repent God of all my sins and I put it all under the blood. In the name of Jesus I rebuke the generational curse of **homosexuality** and **I charge** the spirit of **homosexuality** to come out of me, and enter no more into me in the name of Jesus. It is done!

And he said unto them, This kind can come forth by nothing, but by prayer and fasting (Mark 9:29)

This is an abomination!!!!

AN ABOMINATION TO GOD

For the wrath of God is revealed from heaven against all ungodliness and unrighteousness of men, who hold the truth in unrighteousness; Because that which may be known of God is manifest in them; for God hath shewed it unto them. For the invisible things of him from the creation of the world are clearly seen, being understood by the things that are made, even his eternal power and Godhead; so that they are without excuse: Because that, when they knew God, they glorified him not as God, neither were thankful; but became vain in their imaginations, and their foolish heart was darkened. Professing themselves to be wise, they became fools, And changed the glory of the uncorruptible God into an image made like to corruptible man, and to birds, and fourfooted beasts, and creeping things. Wherefore God also gave them up to uncleaness through the lusts of their own hearts, to dishonour their own bodies between themselves: Who changed the truth of God into a lie, and worshipped and served the creature more than the Creator, who is blessed for ever. A'men. For this cause God gave them up unto vile affections: for

even their women did change the natural use into that which is against nature: And likewise also the men, leaving the natural use of the woman, burned in their lust one toward another; men with men working that which is unseemly, and receiving in themselves that recompence of their error which was meet. And even as they did not like to retain God in their knowledge, God gave them over to a reprobate mind, to do those things which are not convenient; Being filled with all unrighteousness, fornication, wickedness, covetousness, maliciousness; full of envy, murder, debate, deceit, malignity; whisperers, Backbiters, haters of God, despiteful, proud, boasters, inventors of evil things, disobedient to parents. Without understanding, covenantbreakers, without natural affection, implacable, unmerciful: Who knowing the judgment of God, that they which commit such things are worthy of death, not only do the same, but have pleasure in them that do them
(Romans 18:1-32).

CHAPTER 12

LIFE CHANGING PRAYERS

Confess your faults one to another, and pray one for another, that ye may be healed. The effectual fervent prayer of a righteous man availeth much (James 5:16).

PERSONAL PRAYERS

A PRAYER FOR BLESSINGS TO BE RELEASED FROM THE SPIRITUAL REALM

Lord I pray in the name of Jesus that you release my blessings from the spiritual realm right now. I believe in you as well as your word. Through faith all things are possible so, I am confident that you will let the Angels in Heaven get all my blessings that are caught up in the Spiritual Realm and allow them to manifest in the natural unto me in Jesus name. Amen.

> *And this is the confidence that we have in him, that, if we ask anything according to his will, he heareth us: And if we know that he hear us, whatsoever we ask, we know that we have the petitions that we desired of him* (I John 5:14-15).

A PRAYER FOR FORGIVENESS

Jesus please forgive me for all the wrong that I have done in your sight and forgive me for all the hidden and seen unforgiveness in my heart. I repent and I ask you on this day to create in me a clean heart and renew in me a right spirit Lord. Lord, please change my way of thinking. Grant me to have the mind of Christ more and more each day. God as I strengthen my walk in life with you, as I read and abide in your word daily, I ask that you allow me to decrease in all my ways so that I can increase in you with the Holy Spirit guiding me daily. Lord, know that I have asked you for forgiveness. I am asking you for forgiveness in my heart to be able to forgive all of mine enemies, my friends as well as my loved ones for all the things they have done to me and/or against me right now God in the name of Jesus I pray. God I also ask that you cleanse me from all unrighteousness. Then allow your Holy Spirit to be a light in my life so others can see the God in me. I ask right now God that you allow me to have a clean slate with you as I continue to put you first in my life through seeking your face oh God! All these things I ask in your Son Jesus name and I believe in my heart it is done. Amen.

A PRAYER LEADING TO SALVATION

Where do you want to spend eternity in heaven or hell?
Jesus, I ask you to have mercy on me Lord and purge me
with hyssop so that I can be white as snow. I know
throughout my life I made many mistakes that were not
pleasing in your sight. God, I want you to help me change
my life. It is not easy when I try to change, because I
cannot change by myself. I need you God to come into my
life and lead the way for me to follow. I submit myself to
you right now in the name of Jesus! I need you God right
now this very moment, so I am personally inviting you into
my life. God I am all messed up and full of negative
thoughts and unforgiveness in my heart. I want to do what
is right Lord. I will serve you for the rest of my life. God
your word cannot come back to you void so I understand
that I am saved now and have salvation because of what
Romans 10:9-10 says.

*That if thou shalt confess with thy mouth the Lord Jesus,
and shalt believe in thine heart that God hath raised him
from the dead, thou shall be saved. For with the heart
man, believeth unto righteousness; and with the mouth
confession is made unto salvation.*

I believe your Holy word God with my whole heart and now I am able to know without a shadow of a doubt that I am saved. Salvation is a know so and I am now a joint heir according to your promise God because I am Abraham's seed. Lord let your word and your Holy Spirit dwell in me so I can walk by faith and not by sight. Thank God I am saved In Jesus Name, I thank you God. It's done! Amen.

I understand that I must be baptized in Jesus name and I shall receive the gift of the Holy Ghost.

A PRAYER FOR REPENTANCE OF SINS

Jesus, I ask you for forgiveness of all my sins. But before I ask you to forgive me God I understand that I must first go to everyone that I have done wrong to, and have not totally forgiven them and ask them for forgiveness first, then come back to you Lord God. Now at this point God, I am aware that you will hear me by forgiving me for all my sins. I can now repent and go and sin no more JESUS! I know it is hard but your word says in Hebrews 10:26, *For if we sin willfully after that we have received the knowledge of the truth, there remaineth no more sacrifice for sins.* It is understood that in order for your word to really manifest in my life, my Spirit must obey your Holy word to its' entirety and not pick and choose what I will obey and will not obey. I ask you to forgive me God for not obeying all of your word God. I pray right now in the name of Jesus that I am now in your "Perfect Will" for my life God and not your "permissive will". All these things I ask you to put under the blood and not to remember my sins. I repent because I will obey your word from this day forward in Jesus name I Thank you God. Amen!

A PRAYER FOR INCREASE

God, I thank you that you have allowed me to be blessed and prosperous in everything that I do in the name of Jesus. God I thank you for your word, power and your Holy Ghost. From this day forward, everything that I touch with my hands shall prosper in the name of Jesus. Lord, I thank you, praise your name for you are holy, righteous and worthy to be praised. I am a believer of your word, through faith I know you will give me the desires of my heart as long as I put you first in my life. God in Matthew 6:33, your word says, But seek ye first the kingdom of God, and his righteousness; and all these things will be added unto you. In III John 2 your word simply says that, Beloved, I wish above all things that thou mayest prosper and be in health, even as thy soul prospereth. I thank you God for helping me. I will seek your face always because you first loved me. I thank you and praise your Holy name in the name of Jesus. I love you. I am Abraham's seed. I am blessed! I also call down all of my increase and things that have been tied up in the Spiritual Realm to manifest right now in my life "In the Name of Jesus!" I receive it!

A PRAYER FOR PEACE!

Jesus, I thank you first for my life, my health and my strength. I thank you for another day that was not promised. I thank you for allowing me to be in the land of the living one more day God. I thank you right now that you will give me peace that surpasses all understanding. I thank you father God that I am in perfect peace just as your word says in Isaiah 26:3, Thou wilt keep him in perfect peace, whose mind is stayed on thee: because he trusteth in thee. God, since I am a believer of your word and not a doubter. I am in covenant with you God. I am now free in my mind, free in my spirit and able to now usher in your presence into my life so that I can stay grounded and rooted in your Holy Word. No longer will I allow the devil to come into my thought life and hold me hostage from what God has predestined for my life. I cast down every imagination, rebuke all unclean spirits that try to come in my mind. I am now free! God come into my life and take control of my thoughts in Jesus name it is done. No longer will I be led by the powers of darkness. I am a new creature that has been now transformed by the renewing of my mind. Amen.

A PRAYER FOR HEALING

Lord there is healing and power in the name of Jesus! I believe that I can do any and everything that your Holy word says I can do. I know without a doubt in my mind that there is power in the name of Jesus. God your word says in Proverbs 18:21, *Death and life are in the power of the tongue and they that love it shall eat the fruit thereof.* Lord, I believe that by your stripes I am healed in the name of Jesus from all sickness. I thank you God. Let everything that has breath praise the Lord!

A PRAYER FOR FAITH

Lord I thank you and ask you to remove anything in me Jesus that is not like you. Use me as a vessel and an instrument of light to show your people that you are real! God I ask that you allow me to decrease so that your Holy Spirit can increase in me God. Lord I thank you for your Holy Spirit that is leading and directing my path so that I can take a closer walk with you Lord Jesus and be filled with the Holy Ghost more and more each day. Lord I thank you for the truth. Thank you for faith. I am able to walk by faith and not by sight. I thank you God that no matter what my situation looks like, it is not what it appears to be. It is understood that you are the author and the finisher of my faith! Now I can see clearly now and I am able to spread the Gospel of your Holy word into the earth so that your will be done in the earth. In Jesus name I thank you for endurance that I can finally take my eyes off everything else and see you Jesus. I thank you God that you have allowed me to walk by faith and not by sight. I am now able to exercise my faith in you God. I BELIEVE IT AND RECEIVE IT IN JESUS NAME. Amen.

THE PRAYER OF JABEZ

I Chronicles 4:10 And Ja'bez called on the God of Israel, saying, Oh that thou wouldest bless me indeed, and enlarge my coast, and that thine hand might be with me, and that thou wouldest keep me from evil, that it may not grieve me! And God granted him that which he requested. Thank you God for granting me all my requests! In the name of Jesus. Amen.

THE SAVED PRAYER

Thank you Jesus for saving me. I have been delivered from all my sins. Thank you Jesus for caring for me and being so kind enough to save me from the burning pits of hell. Thank you God that I am saved and my salvation is in you Jesus. Now that I am saved, I live my life unto you. I put you first in my life. I thank you for your mercy, grace, peace, love and protection. I thank you for all that you have done for me. Thank you God that I am a new creature. In Jesus name. Amen.

SPEAKING MY BLESSINGS INTO EXISTENCE!

God, I thank you for life more abundantly and for the supernatural in everything that I do. Each day I wake-up in the morning, God I know I am one step closer to receiving all the blessings you have for me as long as I am obedient to your word. Lord God I thank you in advance in Jesus name for blessing me with the desires of my heart. God your word says no good thing will you withhold from me! Also, God your word says you already know what I have need of before I ask. So, God I just want to do your will and be in your perfect will for my life. In Jesus name I call it done and I receive it. Amen. Thank God!

THANK YOU

I thank you God for all you have done for me and for the many times you have spared my life over and over again. I thank you God in the name of Jesus that you have given me life and I thank you for anointing me. God you are so wonderful and I thank you for using me to help show someone that you are God. I thank you God in the name of Jesus for more than enough!

A PRAYER FOR STRENGTH

Lord I thank you for strength. God I thank you that you are making me stronger in spite of all my tests, trials and tribulations. I thank you for all of your mercy, grace, favor, the anointing and the power of God over my life. I thank you LORD GOD IN THE NAME OF JESUS that you continue to strengthen me to be able to withstand all the wiles of the devil and allow me to be rooted, steadfast and unmoveable and grounded in your word. God I thank you that you have given me peace and I thank you for teaching me how to stand on your word and continue to be faithful. Thank you Jesus for strength! Amen.

A PRAYER ON HOW TO LOVE MY ENEMIES

God I ask you to teach me how to love my enemies. Please speak to my heart and allow your unconditional love to come into my heart and spirit right now in the name of Jesus, I ask and pray Jesus. God I love you and I know in order for me to make it into heaven I must love my enemies Lord God. I am asking you right now in the name of Jesus to teach me all of your ways and teach me to love unconditionally and allow your spirit to come upon me and dwell in me. Use me God so you can get all of the glory in Jesus name, Amen.

A PRAYER FOR THE ANOINTING ON MY LIFE

Jesus, I thank you for your sweet spirit and I thank you for your anointing God that you have placed over my life in the name of Jesus. God I thank you for your holy spirit. I thank you God that you have anointed me to spread the gospel in the earth to your people. I thank you Jesus for being with me every step of the way. Lord, I thank you for the anointing that you have placed on my life that destroys every yolk. God I ask that you would now give me a double portion of your anointing and power just as Elisha received from Elijah. Thank you Jesus for not allowing anything to offend me. I thank you God in your Son Jesus name it is done!

A PRAYER FOR THE FAVOR OF GOD

Thank you Jesus for favor and for allowing everything in the Spiritual realm to come down and fall into my hands. I am your child and then a servant to you Lord. I am seeking your face and at the same time I put you first in my life. Jesus, I know that if I am obedient to your word, you will allow for your favor and your Holy Ghost power to come into my life. Jesus, I understand now that you are my source and strength for everything I need in my life. I thank you Jesus for granting me favor. In your Son Jesus name I thank you and I praise your Holy Name God. Amen.

A PRAYER FOR ENDURANCE

And let us not be weary in well doing: for in due season we shall reap, if we faint not (Galatians 6:9).

Jesus, I thank you right now and ask that you give me patience to endure my storms in life. God, I thank you for hearing my cry and answering all of my prayers in advance through your Son Jesus name. In Jesus name, I thank you God because you are an awesome, holy and a righteous God. I glorify and magnify your name because you are worthy of all praises. Thank you for endurance. I thank you right now Jesus for mercy. I thank you for your grace Lord. I thank you for your anointing and your power in the name of Jesus! I ask and pray that you supply all my needs. I thank you for teaching me how to have faith and trust in you Jesus for everything, because I know that my God shall supply all my needs according to his riches in glory, by Christ Jesus. Thank you Jesus for your sweet spirit that abides in me. Thank you Jesus for your deliverance power and your holy word that has allowed me to get through each day. I forever give your name the honor, in Jesus name I pray. Amen.

A PRAYER FOR A "HELP MEET"

Lord, I thank you for allowing me to be in your perfect will for my life. Lord I put all my trust and faith in you because I know you will lead, teach and guide me. Thank you because the Holy Spirit will guide me the right way! I also thank you in advance for keeping all the wolves in sheep clothing out of my presence in Jesus name. Thank you Lord that I will not be unequally yoked with unbelievers like your word says in II Corinthians 6:14, In Jesus name, I call it done!

And Adam gave names to all cattle, and to the fowl of the air, and to every beast of the field; but for Adam there was not found an help meet for him. And the Lord God caused a deep sleep to fall upon Adam, and he slept: and he took one of his ribs, and closed up the flesh instead thereof; And the rib, which the Lord God had taken from man, made he a woman, and brought her unto the man. And Adam said, This is now bone of my bones, and flesh of my flesh: she shall be called Woman, because she was taken out of Man. Therefore shall a man leave his father and his mother, and shall cleave unto his wife: and they shall be one flesh (Genesis 2:20-24).

A SHORT PRAYER FOR DELIVERANCE

Jehovah Tsidkenu, I know you are the Lord my righteous. Thank you God for deliverance from all evil and wickedness, thank you for cleansing me and granting me strength to resist temptation. Thank you for being Jehovah Jireh my Provider. In Jesus name, it is done!

The Spirit of the Lord is upon me, because he hath anointed me to preach the gospel to the poor; he hath sent me to heal the brokenhearted, to preach deliverance to the captives, and recovering of sight to the blind, to set at liberty them that are bruised (Luke 4:18).

And the Lord shall deliver me from every evil work, and will preserve me unto his heavenly kingdom: to whom be glory for ever and ever. Amen (II Timothy 4:18).

INVITATION TO CHRIST

If you want to accept Jesus Christ today, I extend the invitation to you.

Jesus, I repent for all my sins, known and unknown. I come to you asking you to forgive me God by changing me so that I can be made whole. I accept you Lord Jesus as my Savior. Lead me and guide me to be obedient to your word. Help me to come into the knowledge of the truth and have a one-on-one relationship with you Jesus. I ask and pray and call it done In Jesus name. Amen.

Jesus saith unto him, I am the way, the truth, and the life: no man cometh unto the Father, but by me (John 14:6).

If ye had known me, ye should have known my Father also: and from henceforth we know him, and have seen him (John 14:7).

Then Peter said unto them, Repent, and be baptized every one of you in the name of Jesus Christ for the remission of sins, and ye shall receive the gift of the Holy Ghost (Acts 2:38).

I AM SAVED

I, _____, accept Jesus Christ on this day of
_____, in the month of _____in
the year of 20_____.

WELCOME TO THE BODY OF CHRIST!

Remember to: Get baptized in the name of Jesus Christ!

Pray each and every day without ceasing.

Surround yourself with other worshippers.

Fast and pray in the Spirit.

Rebuke the devil in the name of Jesus!

For as the body is one, and hath many members, and all the members of that one body, being many, are one body: so also is Christ (I Corinthians 12:12).

For by one Spirit are we all baptized into one body, whether we be Jews or Gentiles, whether we be bond or free; and have been all made to drink into one Spirit (I Corinthians 12:13).

For the body is not one member, but many (I Corinthians 12:14).

CLOSING PRAYER

I Thank you for sowing a seed into my Book Ministry and I speak total deliverance, healing, peace, mercy, grace, and blessings over your life IN THE NAME OF JESUS! I pray that you receive the revelation that anything you say will manifest in the earth because death and life are in the power of the tongue, and they that love it shall eat the fruit thereof. Praise the Lord!

I PRAY THAT THE ANOINTING AND THE POWER OF GOD FALL UPON YOU ON THIS DAY. IN JESUS NAME. I CALL IT DONE!

AHSRAT PUBLISHING

BOOK AVAILABLE IN ALL STORES

To write the Author, mail to:

P.O. Box 2464

Saginaw, MI 48605-2464

tarsha@tarshaworks.net